AF248692

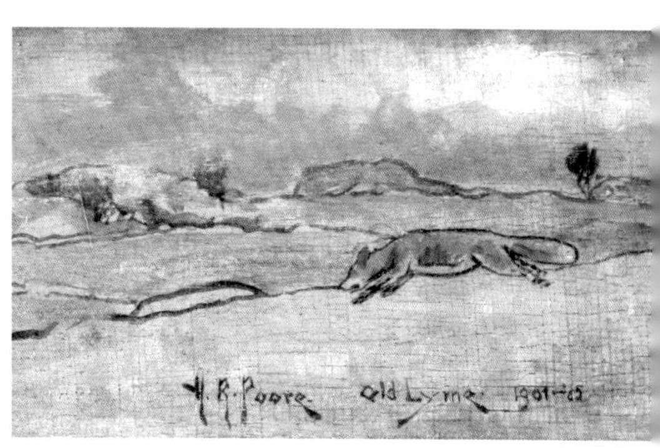
H. R. Poore Old Lyme 1901-02

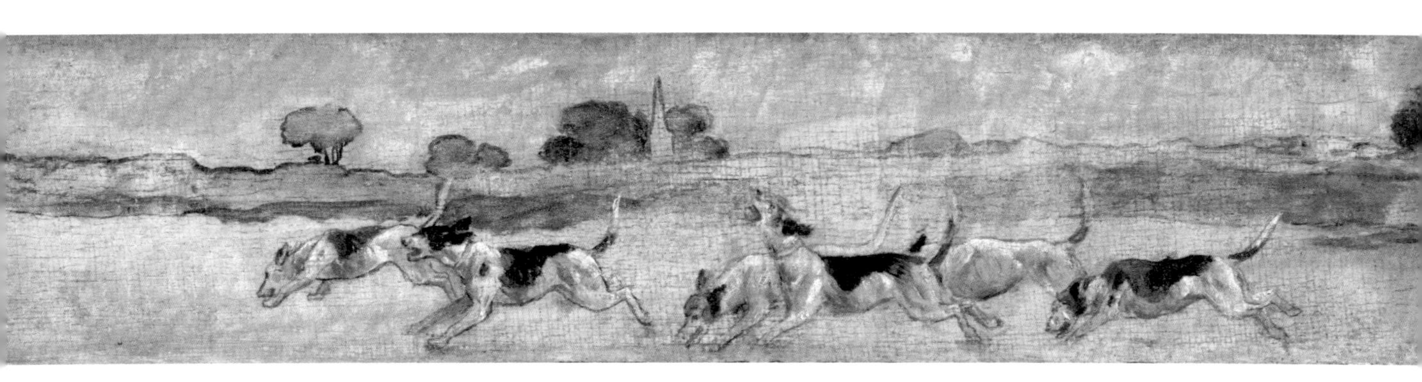

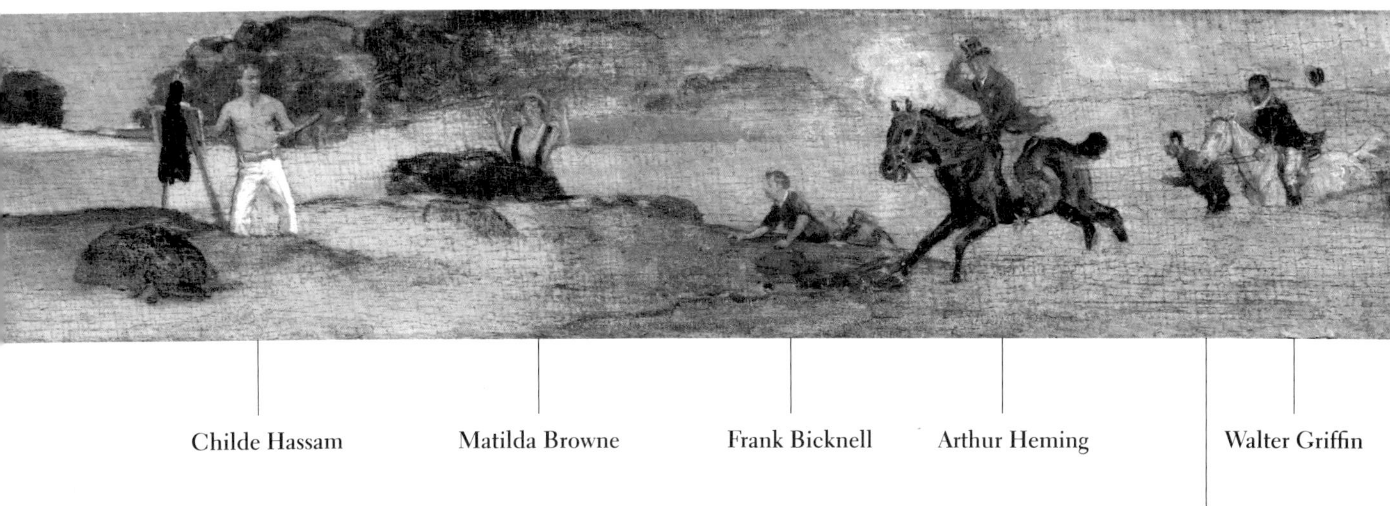

Childe Hassam   Matilda Browne   Frank Bicknell   Arthur Heming   Walter Griffin

William Robinson

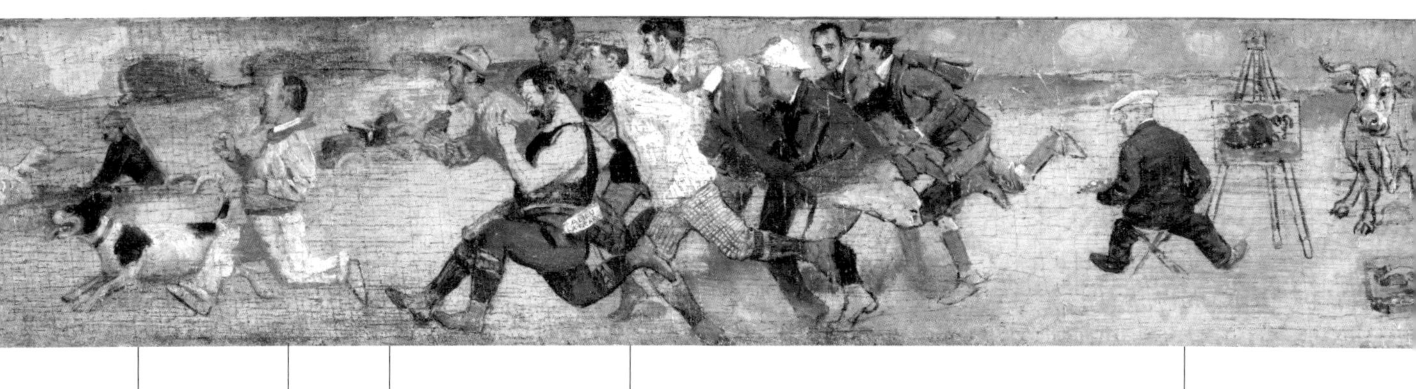

Harry Hoffman

Will Howe Foote

Henry C. White

left to right
Louis Paul Dessar,
Alphonse Jongers,
George Bogert,
Jules Turcas,
Henry Rankin
Poore, Frank
Vincent DuMond,
Cullen Yates,
Allen B. Talcott,
Clark Voorhees, and
Lewis Cohen

William Henry Howe

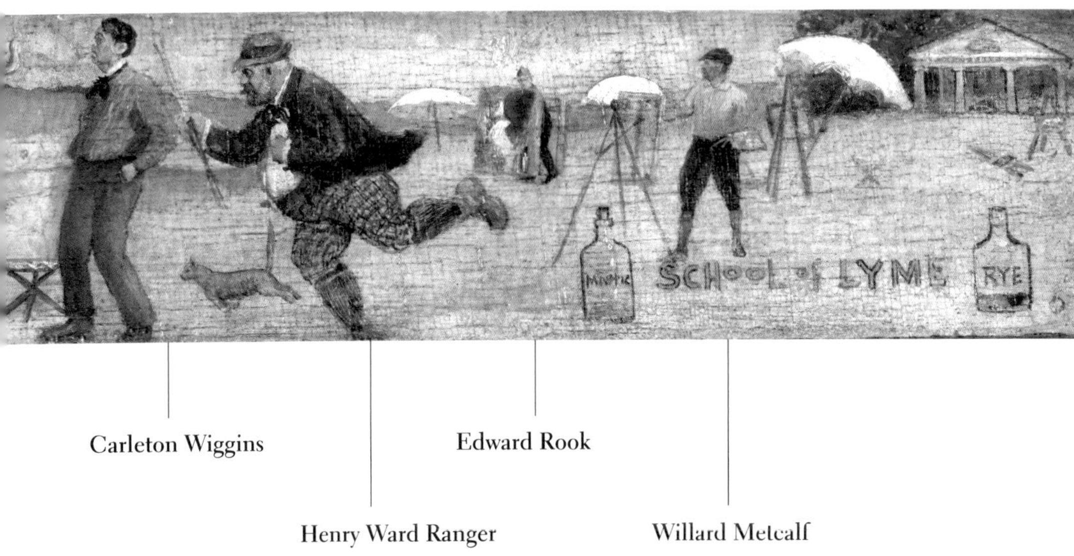

Carleton Wiggins

Edward Rook

Henry Ward Ranger

Willard Metcalf

Henry Rankin Poore, *The Fox Chase*, 1901-05. Oil on wood.
Florence Griswold Museum, Gift of the Artist. The painting features
caricatures of many of the artists mentioned in Heming's story.

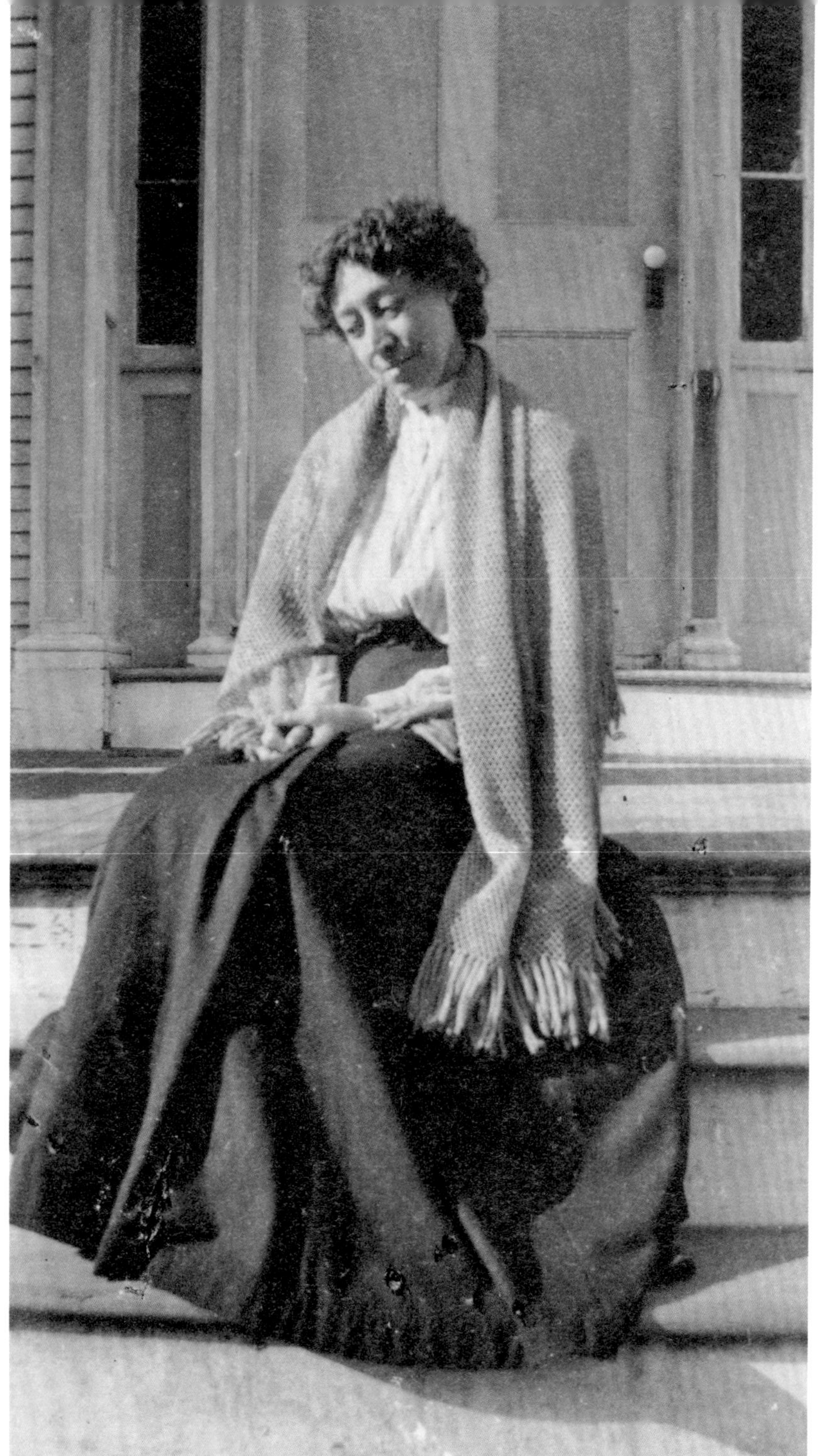

Miss Florence

and

the Artists of Old Lyme

ARTHUR HEMING

ILLUSTRATED BY JAMES STEVENSON

PREFACE TO THE SECOND EDITION BY JEFFREY W. ANDERSEN
FOREWORD BY NELSON C. WHITE

SECOND EDITION

Florence Griswold Museum
Old Lyme, Connecticut

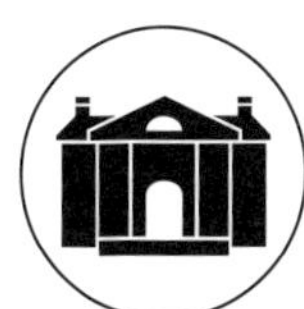

Second edition Copyright © 2013
by the Board of Trustees of the Florence Griswold Museum, Old Lyme, Connecticut.
First edition Copyright © 1971
by Lyme Historical Society – Florence Griswold Association, Inc.

Printed in the United States by GHP Media
Bound by Acme Bookbinding
Designed by Jack Design
Project Editor, Amy Kurtz Lansing, Curator, Florence Griswold Museum

All rights reserved.
This book, or parts thereof, must not be used or reproduced
in any manner without written permission except in
the case of brief quotations embodied in critical articles or reviews.
For information, address the publisher Florence Griswold Museum,
96 Lyme Street, Old Lyme, Connecticut 06371

Library of Congress Cataloging-in-Publication Data:

Heming, Arthur, 1871–1940.
  Miss Florence and the artists of Old Lyme / by Arthur Heming ;
illustrated by James Stevenson ; preface to the second edition
by Jeffrey W. Andersen ; foreword by Nelson C. White. — Second edition.
    pages cm
  ISBN 978-1-880897-24-9 (alk. paper)
1. Griswold, Florence, 1850–1937. 2. Griswold, Florence,
1850-1937—Friends and associates. 3. Painters—Connecticut—
Old Lyme—Biography. 4. Artist colonies—Connecticut—Old Lyme.
5. Old Lyme (Conn.)—Biography. I. Title.
  ND235.O4H4 2013
  759.146'5—dc23
                    2013001971

FRONT COVER James Stevenson, *Arthur Heming arriving at Florence Griswold's house*, 1971.
Ink and wash on paper. Florence Griswold Museum.

OVERLEAF Florence Griswold on the front porch of her house, ca. 1890s.
Lyme Historical Society Archives, Florence Griswold Museum.

BACK COVER Alphonse Jongers, *The Harpist*, 1903. Oil on canvas.
Florence Griswold Museum, Gift of the Lyme Art Association.

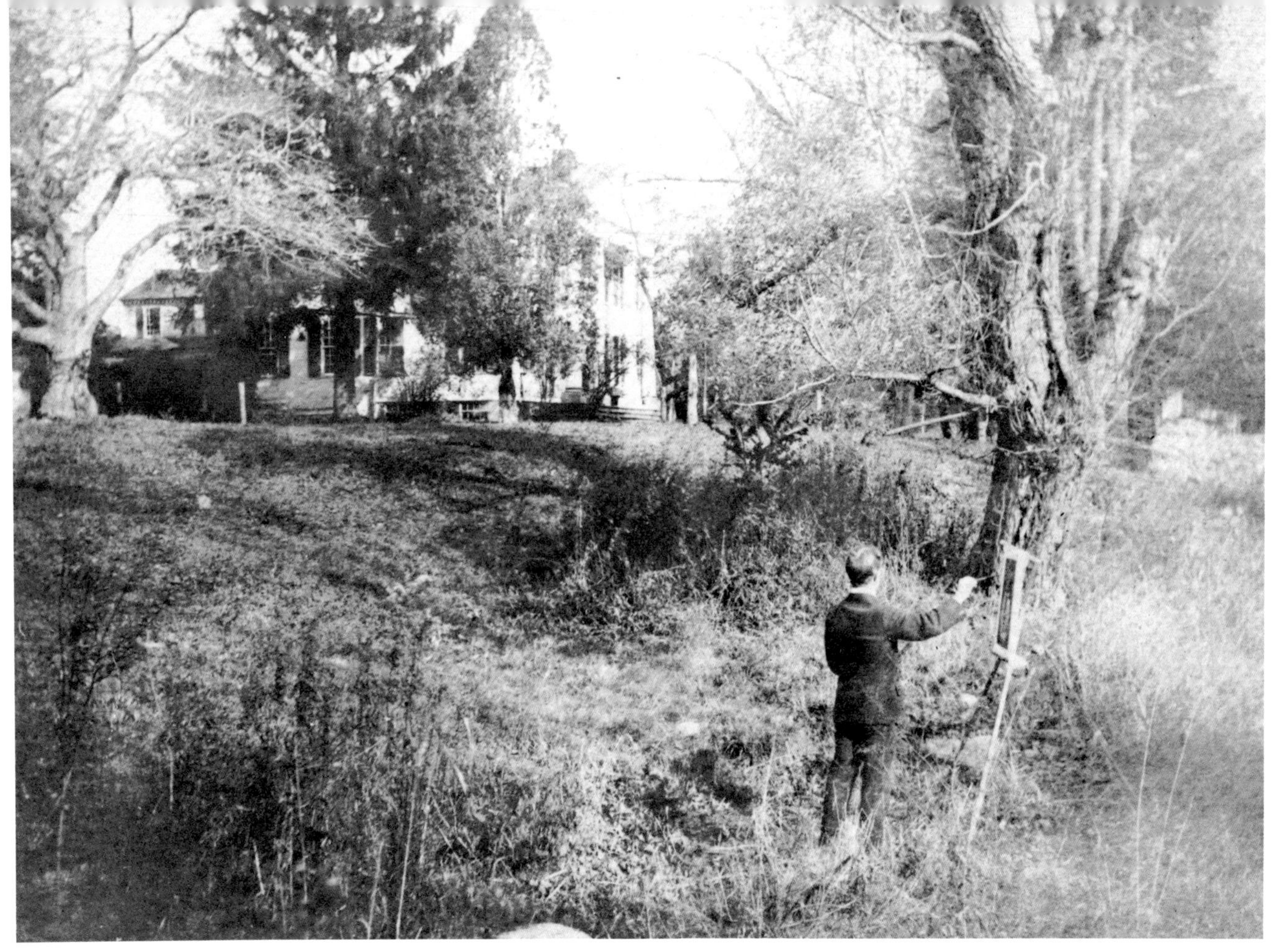

Arthur Heming painting beside the Florence Griswold House, ca. 1904.
Lyme Historical Society Archives, Florence Griswold Museum.

PREFACE TO THE SECOND EDITION

A group of high-spirited artists living together in a boardinghouse is a subject ripe for storytelling, full of amusing incidents and antics from which no one is spared. The Canadian artist, writer, and illustrator Arthur Heming (1870–1940) seized upon this opportunity by writing this valuable memoir of daily life in an American artist colony. *Miss Florence and the Artists of Old Lyme* draws upon Heming's experience of living in the "Holy House," as the artists' boardinghouse was affectionately referred to, during the first decade of the twentieth century. This was a time when the colony was at its height, attracting such leading painters as Henry Ward Ranger, Childe Hassam, and Willard Metcalf, and public figures like Woodrow Wilson. Heming went there initially in 1902 as a student of Frank Vincent DuMond, soon gained acceptance by the other artists (they called him the "Crimson Rambler" for his red hair), and stayed over the next decade to become one of the central figures in the colony, even contributing one of the panels to the famed dining room ensemble within the Griswold House.

Unlike the other artists of the colony, Heming never—at least to our knowledge—painted *en plein air* landscapes of Old Lyme. A formal photograph of him painting outdoors in Old Lyme (p. 63) suggests otherwise but this is probably best viewed as a bit of stagecraft. As an artist, Heming was devoted to portraying Canada as a wilderness paradise for outdoor adventure, which won him an avid following in his native country and abroad. As a lifelong writer, he explored many of these same themes in a prolific series of articles and books, usually accompanied by his own illustrations, that were widely read and viewed. Heming's multiple talents as artist, writer, and illustrator helped to foster Canada's image as "The Great White North" in the minds of American audiences.

But Heming's enduring legacy in Lyme was his uncanny ability to record his memories of the colony's early years with affection and humor. Heming wrote the original manuscript late in life. He began to work on it shortly after the death of Florence Griswold in 1937 and finished it before his own death in 1940. Looking back at events that took place thirty or more years earlier, he vividly recalls them as if they occurred the day before.

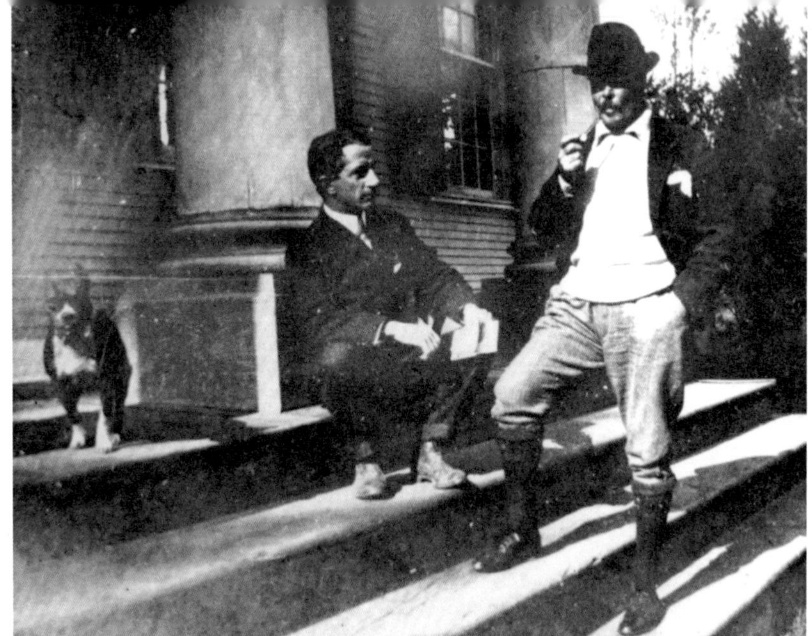

Arthur Heming and Childe Hassam on the steps of the Florence Griswold House, ca. 1903. John L. Hoffman Papers, Lyme Historical Society Archives, Florence Griswold Museum.

While it is true that he took certain liberties to enhance the dramatic narrative there is a basic veracity and authenticity to what he tells the reader. Heming's first-hand account is corroborated by the recollections of other artists and further verified by artist Nelson C. White's original foreword to this book. More than any other account of the colony, Heming succeeds in capturing the personality of the boardinghouse chatelaine Florence Griswold and the essential spirit of her most unusual household that contributed so much to American art history.

It is with this in mind that the Florence Griswold Museum is proud to publish this second edition of a book beloved by its readers and that, until now, has been long out-of-print.

Jeffrey W. Andersen
Director

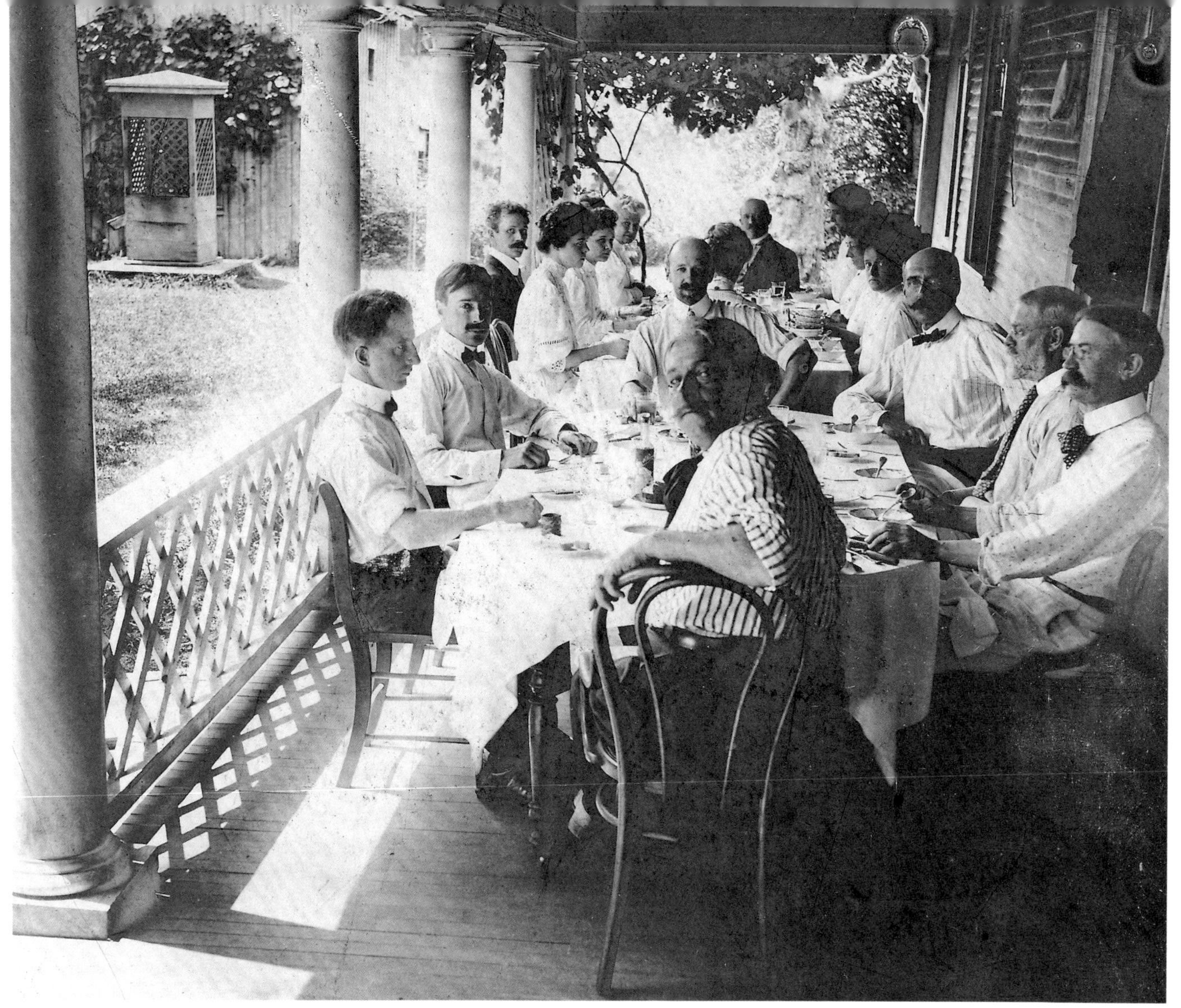

The "Hot Air Club," artists dining on the side porch of Florence Griswold's boardinghouse, 1905. Lyme Historical Society Archives, Florence Griswold Museum.

FOREWORD...

Those familiar with the beautiful town of Old Lyme, Connecticut, have
probably noticed on Lyme Street, not far north of the Route 95 overpass, the
facade of an impressive Greek Revival house with Ionic columns and
graceful proportions. Even today too few people know it as the Florence
Griswold House or realize its artistic and historical importance.

I happen to be one of the few left, perhaps the last, who lived in it when
it was, so to speak, a going concern as a boardinghouse and artists' colony.
I was three years old in 1903 when my parents took me there for a few
weeks in the spring and fall. My father, Henry C. White (1861–1952), was
a landscape painter from Hartford, Connecticut, and through his friend,
Allen B. Talcott, also a landscape painter from Hartford and already a
part-time member of the colony, he was introduced to the Griswold House
and its charming owner, Miss Florence Griswold. In spite of my extreme
youth at the time I still have vivid memories of the Florence Griswold House
and of the artists who went there, for many of them and their wives became
lifelong friends of my family.

So I can testify to the truth and accuracy of Arthur Heming's entertaining
essay of reminiscence which conveys better than anything I have ever read
the spirit of the old house, and of Miss Florence herself who, with her
gentle, cheerful disposition, her gracious hospitality, had such a powerful
influence upon each and every one. As will be seen, it was no mean
achievement to reconcile and keep at peace with one another a group of
highly individualistic and creative men and women who not infrequently
acted like school children. Her optimism was unquenchable and her
personality so persuasive that everyone who went there came under her spell.

It would be impossible in the length or scope of any one book to recount
all of the amusing and memorable incidents that took place during the
years of Miss Florence's life with the artists. It is possible to reproduce only
a sampling of the paintings which were done by some of the most
distinguished of the men who went there. But Arthur Heming admirably
describes the sort of life which went on during those fruitful and happy years.

A word should be said about the many people who, over the years, have contributed time and money to keeping the old house in repair and bringing it back to what it was when Miss Florence inherited it, while carefully preserving the additions and decorations which the artists contributed. Some of the original artists helped greatly to establish it as a permanent institution which now makes it one of the unique landmarks in Connecticut and indeed New England. Notable among those who helped to bring this about were Harry L. Hoffman who was one of the original artist members of the colony, Mr. and Mrs. G. Page Ely, Dr. Matthew Griswold, Mr. Samuel Thorne, Mrs. G. Wells Barney and the current president, Mrs. John Crosby Brown, whose tireless energy has attracted widespread support and who has almost single-handed brought the lovely old house back into the admirable condition in which it is today, and who found Heming's manuscript among some papers when she first took office.

Those who read *Miss Florence and the Artists of Old Lyme* have a most entertaining and inspiring experience in store for them, and, as it is not a fictional account, we can be sure that it is closer to the truth of what happened than, for example, Hawthorne's *Blithedale Romance* about Brook Farm or most other descriptions of attempts at communal living in America's past.

Nelson C. White
Waterford, Connecticut
January 15, 1971

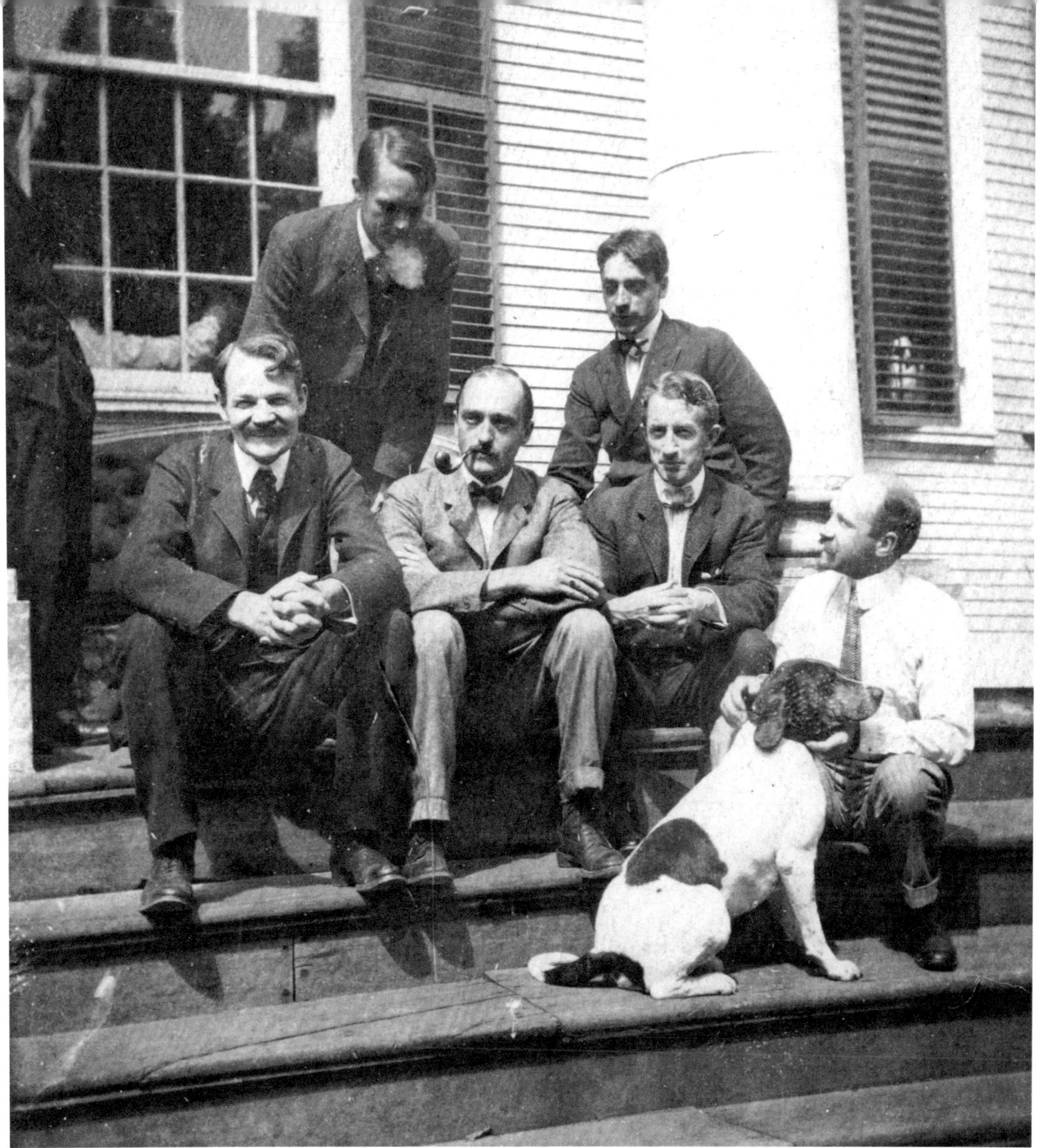

Artists sitting on the porch of the Griswold House, ca. 1904,
(Heming in front row, third from the left).
Lyme Historical Society Archives, Florence Griswold Museum.

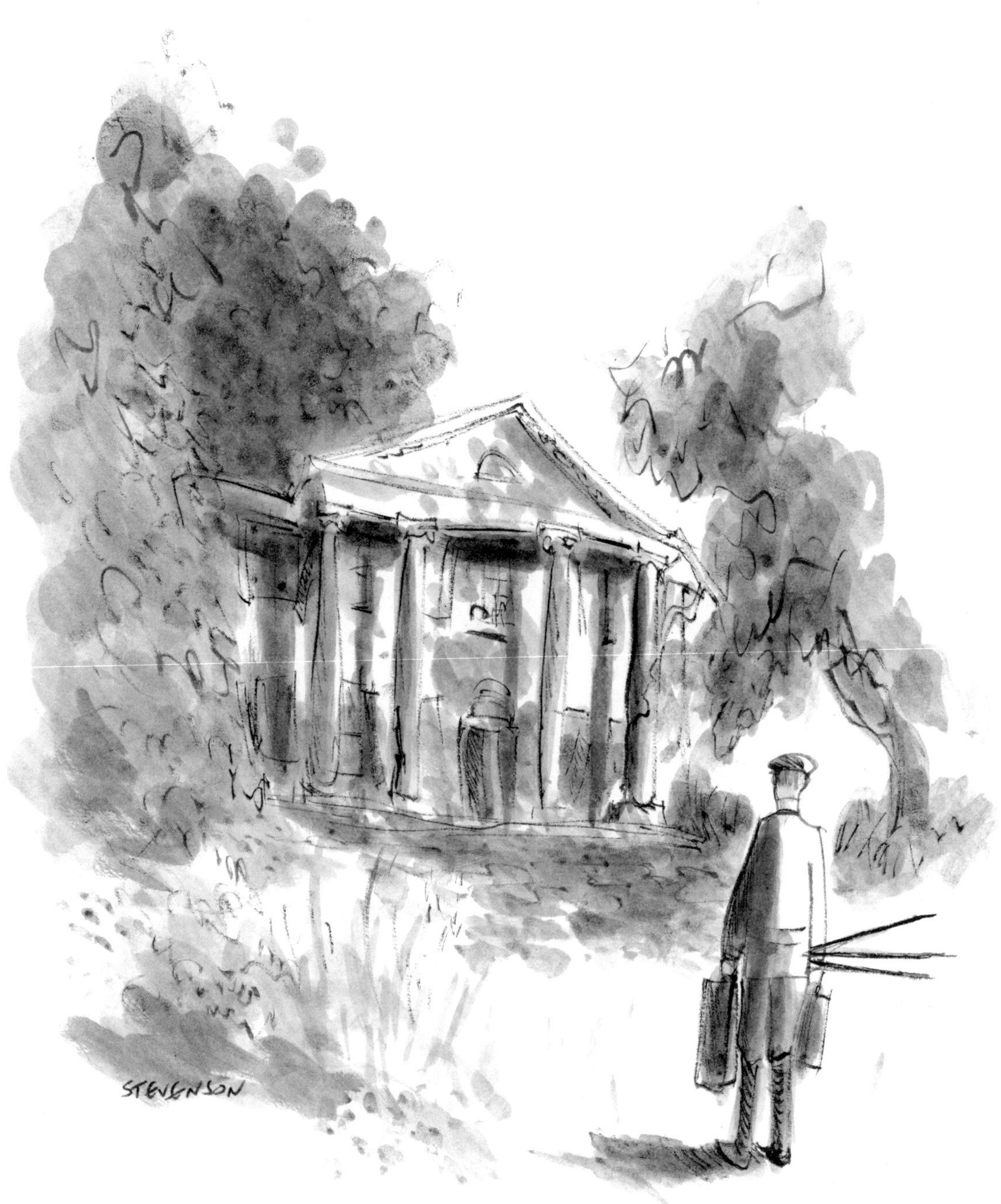

Miss Florence and the Artists of Old Lyme

ARTHUR HEMING

A charming house that appeared like a Roman temple among the trees

On December the 8th, 1937, when I read the editorial in *The New York Times* entitled: "A Lady of Old Lyme," I at once recalled Woodrow Wilson's last letter to me dated 22nd of November 1921, in which he said:

> *"The memory of those carefree days in Lyme is still very fresh with me, and very fragrant."*

For he and his family had often shared her hospitality as did many another whose memory of her will always remain "very fresh and very fragrant."

"Florence Griswold was born on Christmas Day." And as the editorial states, "The next would have been her eighty-seventh. She came into the news and into the hearts of many of us last year when the artists to whom she had been so kind in their hard-up days associated themselves to buy her house, mortgaged to the ridgepole, give her a home for life and then make it a public, as it has long been a private, museum. Their project was defeated but by courtesy of the higher bidder, she was permitted to die in the house where she was born . . . .

"In her delicate and high-bred way Miss Florence had her part in fostering an authentic American art. Fortunately, her painters painted her again and again, and many a down-at-heel artist left on her walls panels on other subjects signed by names that were to become distinguished. So the memory of this gracious and generous spirit survives, and not in Griswold House alone but as part of no inconsiderable chapter in the history of our native art."

How easily I remember my first sight of her home nearly forty years ago.
There amid a setting of sycamores, cedars, elms and willows, with a little
brook in the foreground, I saw a charming house that appeared like a
Roman temple among the trees. Admiringly I beheld the broad steps
surmounted by four huge Ionic columns[1] that towered to the roof and
formed a magnificent adornment to the mansion's front, the handsome old
doorway of which stood hospitably open. But on looking a little closer, a
spirit of sadness enveloped me, when I saw how decay had taken possession
of that beautiful old home. The patched roof, the crumbling cornice, the
decayed pillars, the dilapidated shutters, the rotten steps, and the broken
windows spoke loudly of the ravages of time. Now it seemed to me that it
was but a great tomb crowded to the very roof with the memories of past
generations. For her house had been built in 1817.

[1] *In the original manuscript Heming referred to "Corinthian pillars." In the interest of accuracy this single change to "Ionic columns" was made.*

Against the mildewy and tattered wallpaper in the hall were a number of ancestral portraits

Several times I swung the old doorknocker. But no one came. Then I
pulled the old fashioned bell. Still no one answered. Stepping into the big
hall, I bared my head, seemingly out of reverence to the bygone days that
had been lived in that old home. Then I looked around. There I saw two
old sofas that had gouged holes in the wall plaster with their restless backs,
while their wobbly legs seemed to be vainly reaching out after their
runaway casters, as several cats and dogs slept soundly and breathed heavily
among the chaos of faded and tattered cushions and ripped and gaping
upholstery. A tall, gloomy-looking hat rack with a sprained foot leaned
totteringly far out from the wall and threatened at any moment to cast an
avalanche of old clothing across the hall. For its back was nearly broken
under an almost impossible load of coats and wraps and hats and caps of all

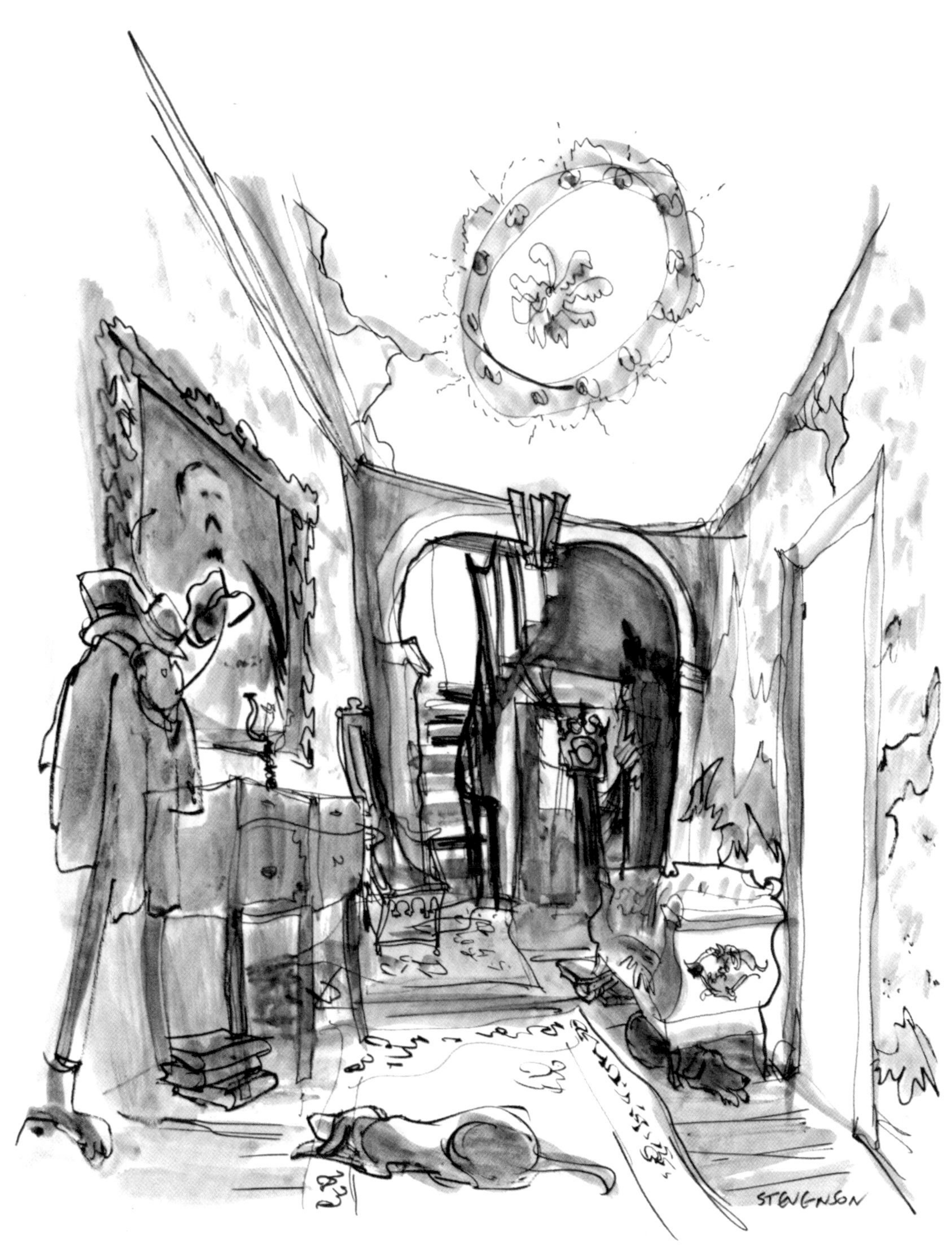

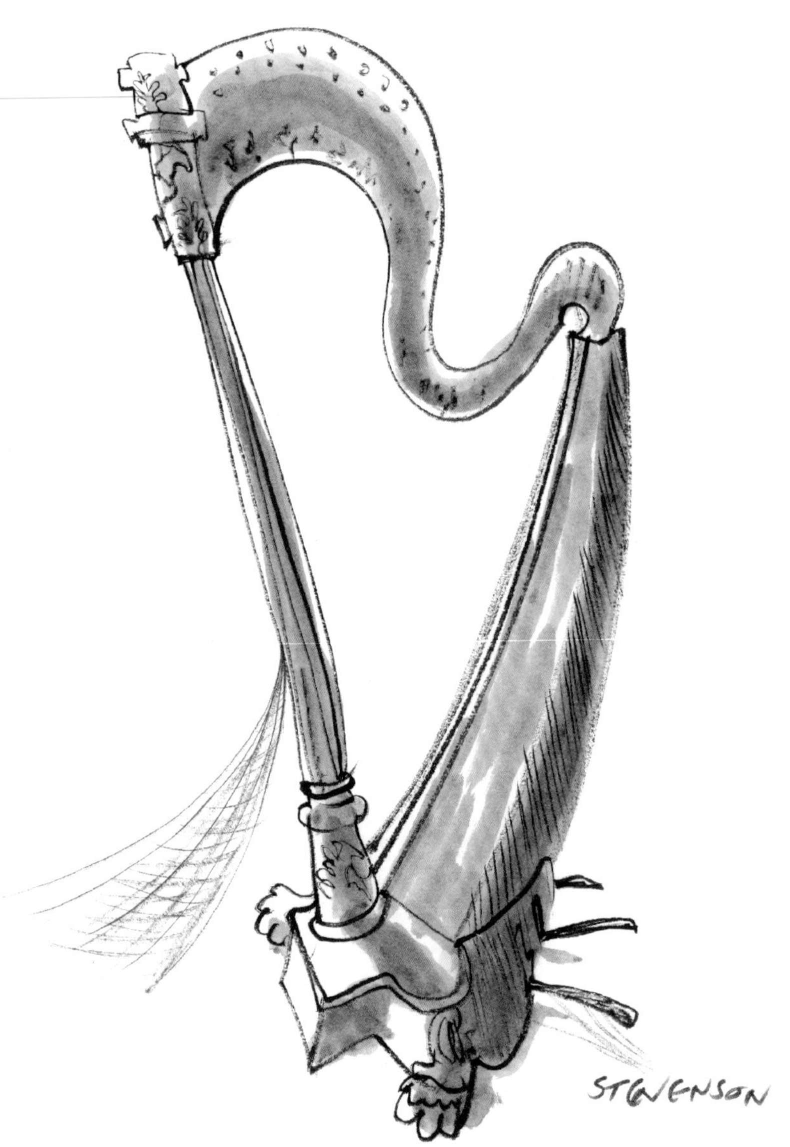

descriptions, some of which looked as though they had hung there for many years. A round table, with one leg dislocated, stood near the front door. A few old chairs with broken backs, rickety legs and uncomfortable seats, stood in corners. Against the mildewy and tattered wallpaper of forty years old design, hung by heavy cords and tassels, were a number of ancestral portraits—for her relations included Governors of States and Chief Justices of the Supreme Court—and minutely painted pictures of clipper-built ships that had sailed the wintry seas between Lyme and London, England, before the days of steam. They depicted how Miss Florence's father, Captain Robert Griswold had been in command, for there, as true as life, was a portrait of him, standing upon the deck, telescope in hand.

A shockingly dilapidated golden harp without a single string

The drawing-room door being open I entered. Its ancient air was somewhat like the hall, only a little worse. Reposing under the broken seat of a handsome old armchair that stood near the center table was a pile of big books to prevent guests from bumping the floor when they sat down. Another pile of books, snuggling under one corner of a splendid old chesterfield, substituted for a missing leg. Another sofa, tilting on its three remaining casters, not only made an unsightly display of its soiled lining where its silken covering had given way, but also thrust into view its hairy padding.

In an alcove stood a piano, and on either side stood a rickety bookcase with its contents stacked helter-skelter upon misplaced shelves. In a corner stood a chest of six or seven overloaded and unclosed drawers that apparently served as Miss Florence's filing cabinet. Near at hand a marble-topped table supported a large bowl in which hovered a couple of sad-looking goldfish that were aimlessly blowing bubbles in the stale water.

On the four window sills rested long flower boxes of rotten wood, still partly covered with patches of wallpaper, and containing a number of almost lifeless, but very tall, dusty, and ancient geraniums that resembled nothing so much as an assortment of old walking sticks. Many other articles of rare old dislocated furniture cluttered the room, and above all rose a beautiful old mantelpiece of chaste design. But heaped upon its shelf was a litter of things entirely out of keeping with its aristocratic character—paint brushes, hat pins, playing cards, pipes, a couple of unfinished sweaters, and a lonely toothbrush.

On the walls hung dingy old steel engravings with glasses broken and frames chipped, while upon the floor, behind the sofas and other odd pieces of furniture, were several beautiful paintings resting against the walls. These, and the three handsomely decorated doors of the room, were the work of Miss Florence's talented boarders. But in the far corner, between the windows, stood what she must have treasured most. It was a once beautiful, but now shockingly dilapidated golden harp, without a single string. Nevertheless, its very presence seemed to speak of her girlhood days when she played it, and which must have been before her father's death, like a golden dream. But even with all its decay and neglect, what an enchanting old home it was.

Not daring to wander any further, I stepped outside and pulled the doorbell again. Presently I heard voices and three people entered the hall's back doorway.

There was my friend, Frank Vincent DuMond, who introduced me to Miss Florence and Henry W. Ranger, the founder of the Lyme art colony. Presently Miss Florence and her friends escorted me around, as I wished to engage a bedroom and a studio for the summer.

"Of course, there's a good deal of repairing and fixing up to do, but then," Miss Florence added, as hope seemed to flash upon her face, "this is going to be a splendid season. In fact the very best I have ever had. So many artists are coming. Indeed, the house will be crowded, and before winter comes, I'll have enough money to restore everything to its former order.

I'm going to have the house shingled and painted, the blinds all fixed up, the verandas mended, and the steps repaired. I'll have all the rooms papered and painted, the furniture overhauled and recovered and some nice new rugs in place of these worn-out carpets. Now just you wait and see if it doesn't all come true. And oh, won't it be perfectly lovely!"

"You evidently believe in wishes coming true," I smiled.

"Indeed I do. Especially if one never grows faint hearted. Anyway, even if our dreams don't come true, we still have the pleasure of hoping they will."

How easily I remember her as she was that day. She wasn't beautiful. She wasn't strong. She wasn't self-reliant. But though they said she was sixty, she didn't look fifty. Her graying, wavy, black hair swept loosely back into a low coil, her well-marked eyebrows, her slender nose, her delicately modelled chin, her sensitive mouth, and her smiling black eyes, these were the features we all remembered. Already I could see she was a born hostess, with that lovely air and remarkable gift of making her guests feel that it was their home, and she was visiting them. And one seemed to feel that sunshine followed her wherever she went—perhaps because she was forever trying to help others.

The bedrooms on the second floor were spacious chambers, each with a fireplace and three or four long windows. They were furnished with four-poster beds, quaint tall mirrors, highboys, what nots, and curious old lambrequins and window decorations.

"You see, everything savors of the past," remarked Miss Florence.

"It certainly does," replied the jovial Henry Ranger, "but when one of those old canopy beds falls down under the combined weight of some unsuspecting lion and his mate, his startled wife always swears it tastes more like dust."

Those were the rooms of the married people. Then up another flight of stairs she led us to the bedrooms of the bachelor men and the bachelor women.

"Oh goodness!" she suddenly exclaimed. "This is going to be a dreadfully busy day for me. I positively don't know which way to turn.

There's the shopping to do, letters to write, directions to give, and right on top of it all there's so many people coming this week I don't know where to put them all. But let me see, I'll give Gifford Beal and Allen Talcott rooms up here. Let me think . . . is this the sixteenth or seventeenth?"

"It's the nineteenth," smiled DuMond.

"Goodness gracious, then Mr. and Mrs. Poore are coming today. My, how I'll have to fly around to get their room ready. But Mr. Heming, would you like to see the studios now? We've got time before lunch."

Around the northeast corner of the house she led us into a wild, forgotten garden where tumbledown arbors and rotting summerhouses stood forlornly among a tangle of weeds and flowers, vines and trees, and the wild chirping of birds seemed to bespeak that it was the hunting ground of Miss Florence's cats.

Out beyond the servants' wing were the woodshed, the barn and the stable. In the flower garden, the orchard, the melon patch and the pasture stood a number of small frame buildings, each with a large businesslike north window. These were the workshops of Miss Florence's large family of grey-haired boys. We looked them all over and then down to the river we went. Three old rowboats were lying near the homemade wharf. Across the square stern of the smallest was painted its name: "The Smallpox." Another, painted red, was called "The Scarlet Fever," and the third was christened "Prickly Heat." Crossing the pasture we examined the little brook where a large willow tree had been blown down. Its trunk was over three feet thick.

"If you like, Miss Florence, I'll cut it up for you," I offered.

"Oh how kind! I'll get James, the gardener, to hunt up an axe for you."

"I've two of my own in my trunk," I said.

Presently "Whistling Mary," a tall, deep-chested waitress standing at the kitchen door, raised a two-foot-long tin horn, and blew such a blast that not only did every artist sketching for a mile around instantly know that lunch was ready at "The Holy House," as the students called it, but so also did the villagers along Main Street, the farmers among the rock-bound hills, and even the fishermen away out on Long Island Sound.

After lunch I devoted the rest of the day to getting settled in my
bedroom and studio.

A blast from a two-foot-long tin horn told every artist for miles around that lunch was ready

Overnight the weather had changed and a gusty rain was falling. At seven
o'clock, the painters' usual breakfast time, Clark Voorhees, Gifford Beal,
Will Howe Foote and I entered the dining room. Of all the rooms in the
house, this was the most interesting. It was really a gallery of art. On its
walls and doors over thirty charmingly painted panels were displayed. Like
the decorations in the hallway and drawing-room, a number were signed by
distinguished names. And all had been gratuitously done out of friendship
for Miss Florence. Childe Hassam had painted the kitchen door, and some
day that dingy old door might sell for more than many a fine house has
brought. And the decoration over the fireplace by Henry R. Poore contains
amusing and lifelike caricatures of many an artist in this story.

Even without those interesting paintings how quaint the room appeared,
with its old-fashioned fireplace with ovens on either side. Along the
plate rail and in curious corner cupboards was displayed a collection of
fine old china.

"Good morning, gentlemen!" Childe Hassam exclaimed as he walked
in, and we turned to see a spruce-looking man of medium height and
powerful build, with a clean-shaven face except for two little dabs on his
upper lip, a mode of hirsute adornment worn by him years before Charlie
Chaplin made it the fashion for the British Army. Hassam was, as we
all know, an artist of high rank and was the original leader in America of
impressionistic art.

"By Jove, a fire would go good this morning," he said as he took an orange from the breakfast table and suggested a game of catch. As we warmed up, faster and faster flew the sphere, until Hassam fumbled, and the orange, amid a clatter of glass, disappeared through a window. Hardly had we time to feel shocked and penitent, when in came Miss Florence. But when we explained, apologized, and offered repairs, she smiled forgivingly and said:

"No, no, boys. I won't hear of it. Not for a single moment. Why, to tell the truth, it's just exactly what I've been longing for. The windows are too tight to open easily. I do so love fresh air. And now that broken pane will let in a breath of spring, and afford just the ventilation the room needs."

"Oh, Miss Florence," smiled Voorhees, "one would believe from the way you talk, that you regarded us lobsters as public benefactors." Then turning to us he added: "But that's just her little habit of turning rotten luck into good fortune."

"But boys, what difference does it make?" Miss Florence replied as in walked William S. Robinson. "I'm going to have a wonderful season this summer. I'm going to make a lot of money. Next winter I'm going to fix up the house. I'll get a big new cooking range for the kitchen. A new rug for this room. The furniture all overhauled. The woodwork painted and new shades for the windows," and with a smile of radiant joy she added: "Won't it look perfectly lovely!" Then away she gaily floated—apparently on the tips of her toes—out into the kitchen, to tell "Barefoot Mary," the cook, to hurry breakfast.

"Yes . . . and she actually thinks it's all coming true!" Robinson deplored. "It's getting on my nerves. When I first came here, I too used to hope, just to keep her company, but year after year of it, and nothing improving . . . blast it, I'm through! For never in this world will she get the price! She's so foolishly kind-hearted. Any old tale of woe will loosen her purse strings. She's always in debt, and always will be right up to her very eyebrows. How she manages to keep afloat the Lord only knows. Worse still, every blessed thing about the place is going to rack and ruin. The roof's leaking.

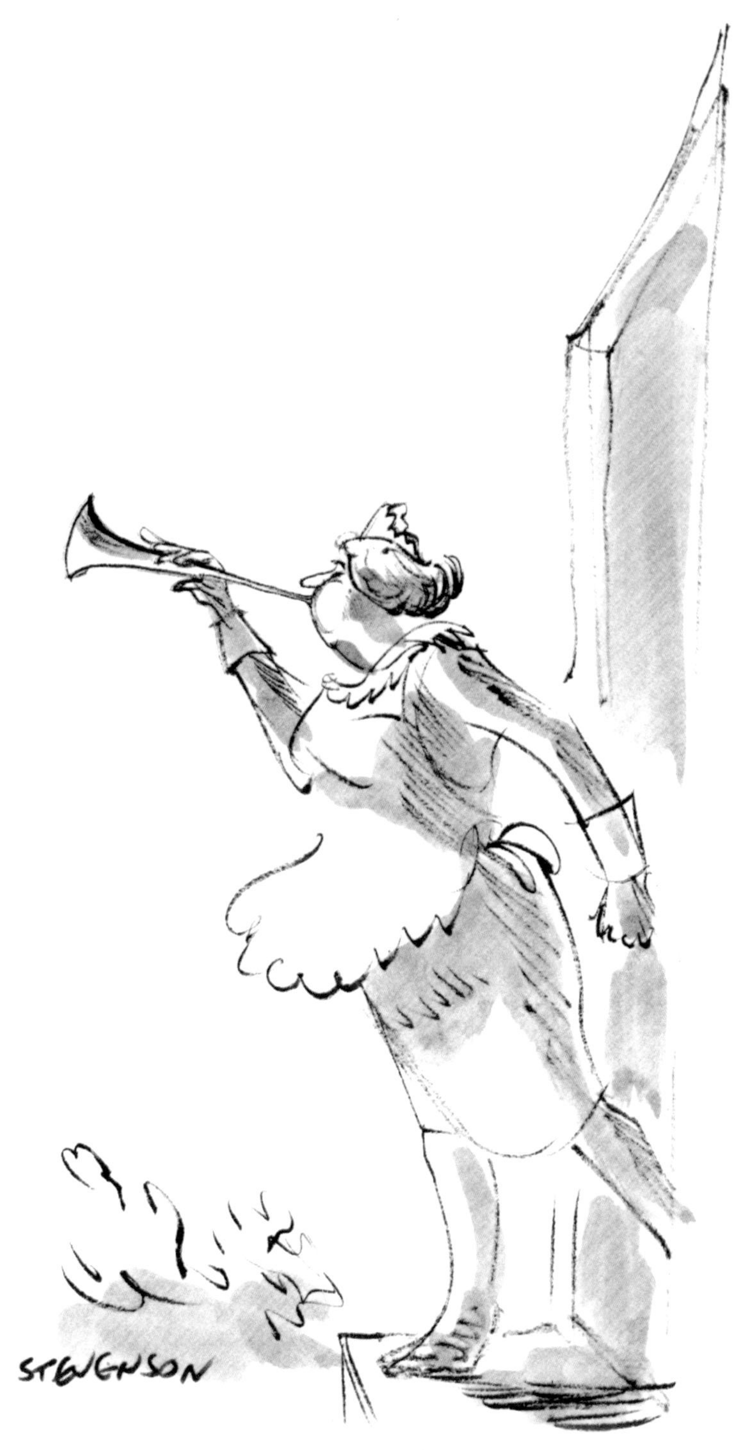

The shutters falling off. The veranda's tottering. The porch pillars
crumbling. The steps giving way. The windows broken. The plaster coming
down. The wallpaper mildewing and peeling. The paint cracking and
chipping. The chairs wobbling. The upholstery ripping. And the carpets—
what's left of them—are nothing but strings and tacks! Blast it! It makes me
blue as the devil and I'm sick of it. For the village people tell me she's been
singing that same old song for over thirty years: 'I'm going to have a
wonderful season. Then I'll have my house all fixed up, and oh, won't it
look perfectly . . .'" Suddenly Robinson stopped as Miss Florence re-
entered the room.

She was carrying a large pot of coffee and behind her came her maids
Margaret and Whistling Mary with arms full of food and arms full of wood.
Matilda Browne and Lydia Longacre had now joined the men, and as the
food steamed and the fire roared, all sat down, and everyone—including
"Wild Bill" Robinson—was happy now. Then "Old Kate" came thudding
into the room to pass around the morning's mail. She walked as though her
feet had been amputated and she was treading on the stumps of her legs.
So heavily did she pound around that she made the dishes and silverware
jingle. But she no sooner appeared than stopped with a jerk and blatted:

"Top o' the mornin' to yez all . . . did yez know that Tait McKenzie came
last night? O' there's Mr. Hassam, the old divvil!"

All laughed, for Old Kate was a character and a privileged domestic.

"Oh Katie," pleaded Miss Florence, both amused and annoyed. "How
can you speak with such disrespect?"

"Aw, now Miss Florence, don't scold me. Mr. Hassam likes it. An'
anyway I did hear Mr. McKenzie sneakin' up the stairs long after midnight.
He must o' come on th' steamer."

Then five cats entered the room, one sinking its claws in my leg. I gave
it so loud a slap that it sounded like a half-filled hot water bottle, and
instantly all the felines raced helter-skelter through the veranda doorway
as Willard Metcalf entered.

"Confound those blasted cats!" he growled. "Miss Florence, they're
driving the birds away!"

That, to Metcalf, was the last straw. He was a big man with well trimmed gray hair and pointed beard, and wore rolled up shirtsleeves, riding breeches and leather leggings. He reminded one of a big Russian general with field glasses slung over his shoulder, for he had already been using them to study the birds. He was the author of many paintings of fine repute and a number of excellent murals.

"What a lark!" exclaimed Miss Florence. "Listen, boys, here's a letter from a lady who spent a summer with me years ago, when I was keeping a girls' school in the winter time. It was before she was married, and now she writes to know if I will chaperon her daughter for the summer. She says Beatrice is rather run down from too many dinners and dances, and ought to have a rest from the social whirl. Mrs. Pope would like her daughter to summer in a country place like mine where there are no men. Now boys, if Miss Pope takes after her mother, she'll be perfectly charming. So it's up to you boys to decide. Shall we have Miss Pope?"

"Certainly." "By all means." "But don't let her know the house is now filled with artists."

"Danger, danger!" Miss Florence warned, playfully shaking her finger at Frank A. Bicknell, a tall, handsome bachelor.

On opening a letter from my artist chum Harry L. Hoffman who had to remain in New York because he couldn't afford to spend the summer in Lyme, I read: "Have just been offered good pay to pitch for a professional baseball team. Shall I accept?"

I had coaxed him to come to Lyme where he would be among a lot of strong painters and thus would have a chance to further strengthen his work. While I was wondering what I could do to bring it about, in walks Tait McKenzie the sculptor and sits down beside me.

"Any particular work on hand?" I asked.

"Yes, an order to do the figure of an athlete."

"Got a model?"

"No, and I'm worried. I suppose I'll have to get one from New York and keep him here all summer."

"I have a painter friend, a Yale athlete, who wants to come to Lyme
to paint. He's a fine figure. What could you pay him?" And I showed
McKenzie a photo of Hoffman.

"Bully! He'll do fine."

Then I went to DuMond, who had a big class of students and wanted to
have his Saturday afternoon lectures taken down in shorthand. I told him
about my chum, that he was going to pose for McKenzie, and that he
could write shorthand.

"Besides," DuMond agreed, "I'll make him monitor of my class and
pay him."

So that too was settled. Then I asked Miss Florence what she would
charge Hoffman for board and have an extra bed put in my room. The
price she mentioned settled all my troubles, and I telegraphed Harry to
come at once. When he arrived he declared:

"Art, I'm going to work hard all summer, and steer clear of girls. In fact,
I'm not going to have anything to do with them."

Everyone liked him and soon he was hard at work, even to helping me
chop up the fallen willow. One afternoon when we were whacking away
among its branches a young lady drove up the lane, and Harry smiled:

"Very nice looking."

"Miss Pope, your trunk is coming up"

Olive-skinned Harry seemed to admire her light hair and fair complexion.
When the carriage stopped in the back yard, Miss Florence came out
to greet her. Minutes later a wagon from the station brought her trunk,
the driver looked around for Old James the gardener, but not seeing him,
the driver dumped the trunk on the grass and drove away. Presently
Miss Florence came out, looked for Old James, too, then she asked if we

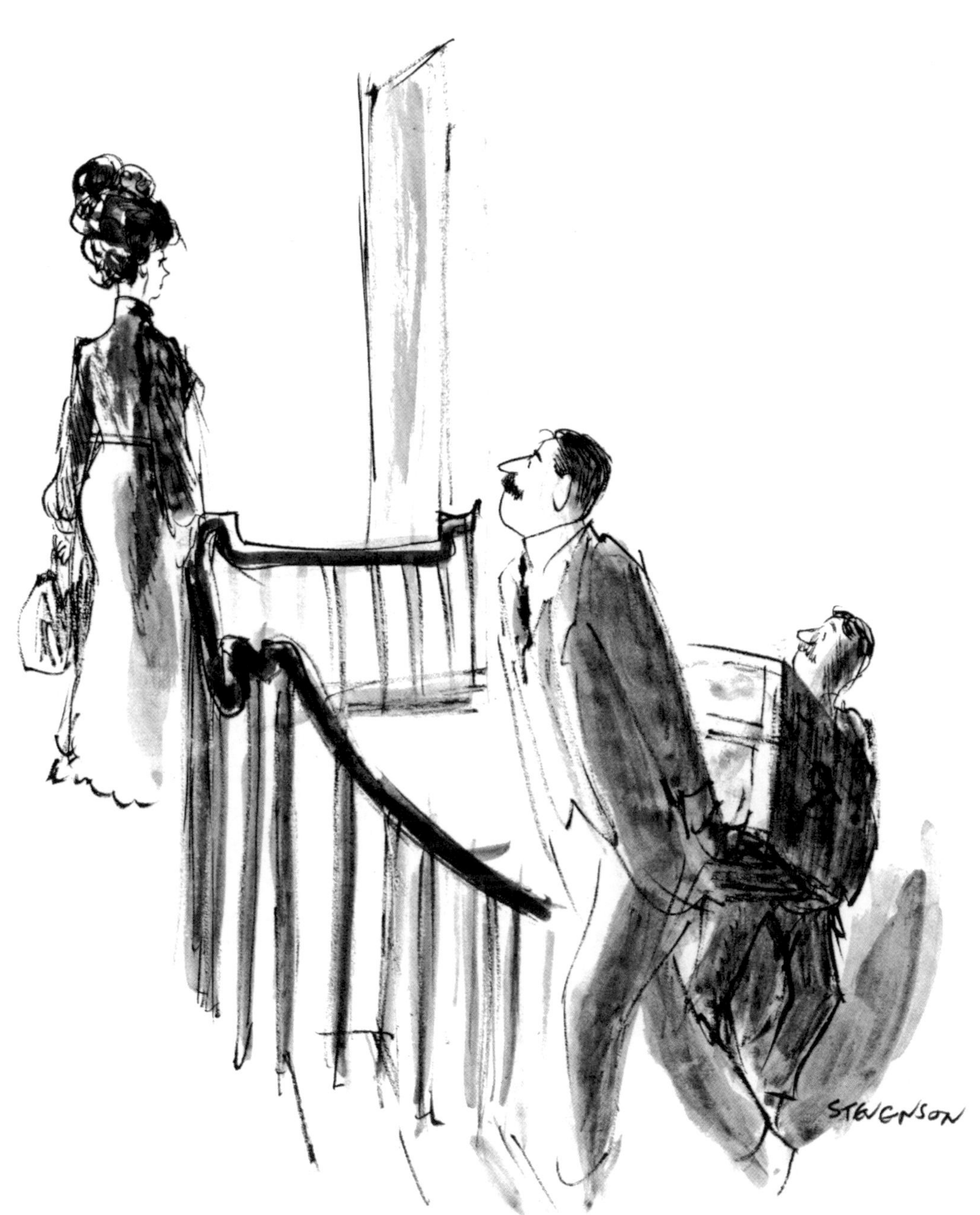

would be kind enough to carry up Miss Pope's trunk, and calling up
the stairs she said:

"Miss Pope, your trunk is coming up."

The young lady was standing near the window, and the late afternoon
sun was casting a golden halo about her head. So enchanted was Harry that
he forgot he was a porter, and paused to feast his eyes.

"Please put it down at the foot of the bed."

But Harry remained entranced.

"Please put it down," she pleaded.

As I was holding the stern end of the trunk I gave it a yank to bring him
to, and at last the trunk came down.

When Miss Florence introduced us at dinner, Harry started leaning
across the table and kept on leaning until Miss Pope promised to go
canoeing with him that evening. Past moonlit marshes, shadowy banks, and
overhanging trees they glided until the little Lieutenant River widened into
a tiny lake that filled a rocky basin and so perfectly reflected the sky that
they seemed to be floating about the stars. Then Harry raised his flute, and
"Lo, hear the gentle lark!" filled the romantic valley with wondrous charm.

Evening after evening they drifted along, until the eighth night when
Harry returned unusually late, and announced his engagement. After we
congratulated him and wished him all happiness, he moaned:

"But how on earth can I ever make enough to marry her?"

"Don't worry. Just be happy. For anyone can see that you are both in love
with each other, and that's all that matters now."

Then I remembered: "Art, I'm going to work hard all summer and steer
clear of girls. In fact, I'm not going to have anything to do with them."

And Mrs. Pope had been so careful to send her daughter "where there
are no men."

Now Beatrice had to write her mother and say: "I'm engaged."

The next day Henry R. Poore from East Orange, N.J., arrived, and when
he heard of Harry's engagement he exclaimed:

"What, Hoffman engaged to Miss Pope? Why they're wealthy—butler
and everything!"

But thank heaven Harry didn't hear it, as Mrs. Pope had invited him to call upon her in East Orange. Their meeting, of course, was a happy one too, and Mrs. Pope returned with Harry.

"Is there any place around here that Harry and Beatrice like best of all?"

"Yes, that hill over there. They both think it is beautiful."

"Then let us drive over there."

Her groaning, shuffling ancient mare, and a rickety, rumbling rattletrap

When we reached the summit and Mrs. Pope saw the little stream running around its foot, and then looked for miles around, she too thought it beautiful. The next day she bought it, twenty-one acres. Then the three of them began to concentrate upon the plans for a suitable house to crown that lovely little hill. And there Harry and Beatrice have lived happily ever after, and son John is now off to college. And if it hadn't been for Miss Florence, would they have ever met? But Harry did her many a good turn too, and twenty-eight years later, when she was about to lose all and be cast out of her own house, he served as treasurer of that very fund the artists raised and which resulted in her dying happily in her old home in which she was born.

One time Miss Katharine Abbott, the author of a number of books on the landmarks of New England, was a guest, and as she wanted to see the surrounding country, Miss Florence offered to show her some of the highways and byways of the district.

Immediately after lunch Old James hitched up ancient Bessie and left her under the big locust tree waiting for the ladies. What a picture they made as Miss Florence and her old mare shimmied down the lane! Bessie with her scrawny, out-stretched neck, her run-over knees and turned-in toes,

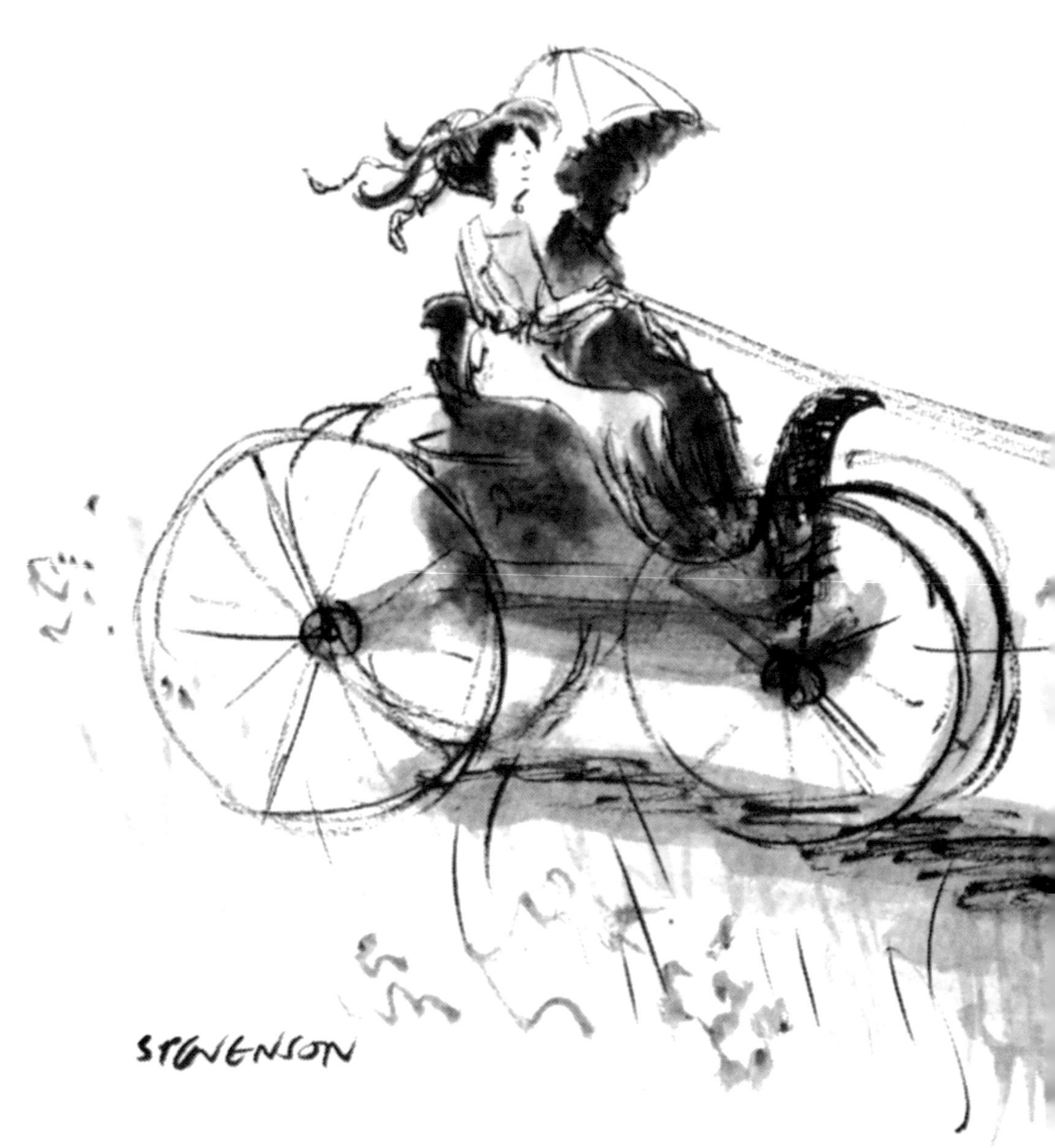
STEVENSON

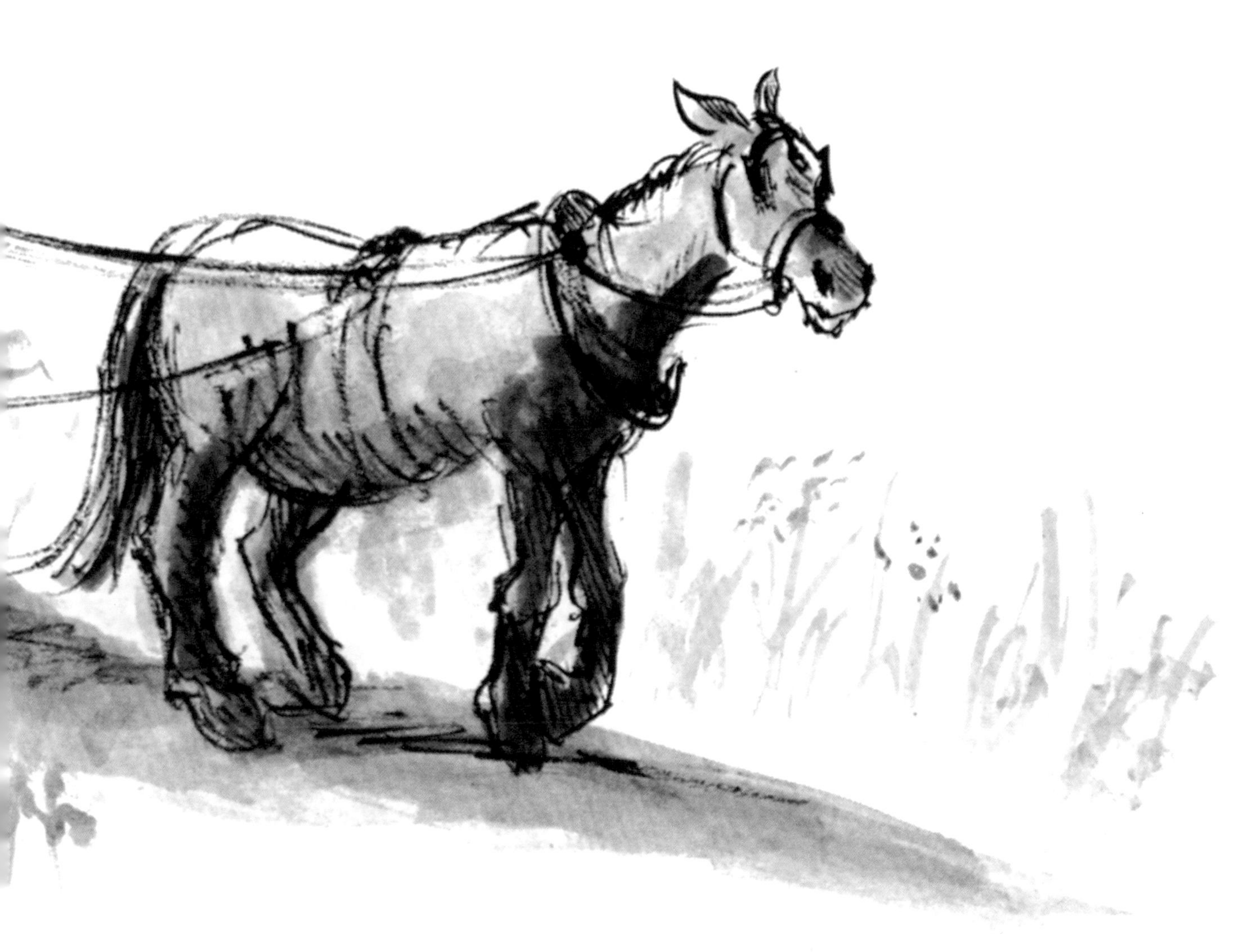

her rusty broken harness patched with baling wire and string; and the equipage, with its loose dashboard, wobbly wheels, and the loose metal fixtures on either side of the box that told of its once tassel-bedecked cover that had long ago vanished forever. Yet with as much dignity and elegance as though driving a high-stepping hackney tandem, Miss Florence drove her groaning, shuffling, ancient mare, and a rickety, rumbling rattletrap. And there she sat, her slender girlish figure in a handsome pale blue silk gown that was twenty years out of vogue. Lace half-mitts encased her timeworn hands. An old-fashioned, broad-brimmed leghorn hat, with silk streamers flowing down behind, crowned her head.

As they slowly drifted along Miss Florence pointed to something of interest with her broken whip, and Miss Abbott made a note of it. Several hours later while on their homeward way a soft sandy road caused a sudden halt on the upward slope of a little hill. After a reasonable rest, Miss Florence applied the whip, and Bessie made an heroic lunge to budge the wheels, but her hame strap broke, her belly-band gave way, and slipping out of her harness, she stood upon the roadside looking quite worried—perhaps because she felt so naked. After a pause of speechless surprise, Miss Florence got out to search under the seats.

"It's just a broken strap. I'll get something to fix it."

But her search was in vain. For some unheard-of reason Old James had for once swept the rig out clean, not even a tie strap remained. Now they were in a fix. There was no help at hand, not even a house in sight. Reharnessing Bessie, Miss Florence backed her between the shafts, and stood pondering as to how the hames could be fastened. Minutes passed, then, a brilliant thought. Sitting down upon the roadside she removed the laces from her boots, and presently the hames were tied.

Once more Bessie lunged and soon they had mounted the hill. But later when they came to sand again, Bessie's necklace broke. Again they were in a plight, for no help or shoelaces were insight, as Miss Abbott wore button boots. At first Miss Florence thought of walking to some farm house, but upon a deep sandy road, in unlaced shoes, that was out of the question.

Then she considered taking them off, but that would wear holes in her stockings, and it would hardly do for her to go barefoot. Indeed Miss Florence was stumped. Once more she pondered. Then another brilliant thought. Bidding Miss Abbott keep watch both ways, Miss Florence stooped over, then she reached way up, and at last withdrew a mysterious article. In a few minutes the hames were once more fastened, and they were homeward bound.

Later, when I heard Bessie rumbling up the lane, I put down my brushes and went out to turn the wheel and hold the steed as the ladies alighted. There came Bessie, looking rather embarrassed as she wore that unmentionable pale blue article upon her chest, and when she saw me coming she let out such a terrific groan that the ladies escaped before I had the courage to ask any questions.

One sultry day four bachelors, revolting at wearing coats while sitting among the ladies in the hot dining room, secured Miss Florence's permission to have a table of their own on the veranda. Then the married men, jealous of the liberty enjoyed by the coatless bachelors, insisted on going out too. A few days later, the women—not to be outdone—also followed suit. Thus the men and the women were not divided, and since that day they have so remained. But as we were now dining on the veranda, the cats behaved worse than ever.

"How many cats have you now, Miss Florence?" Hassam enquired.

"Oh, I'm not quite sure, but I'm sorry to say, not as many as I used to have. Still there's a goodly few."

"Several years ago," volunteered DuMond, when Miss Florence was out of hearing, "there were twenty-eight, as Doctor Sabine can swear, as he supplied the poison. But now, worse luck, it seems all his work has gone for nothing. For Margaret says there are now sixteen. It seems Miss Florence is the fairy godmother of every darned old cat and dog in this region. And they seem to pass the word along, that if any of their pals want a nice tasty dinner or a happy home, they ought to interview Miss Florence."

"She not only treats cats and dogs that way," Hassam added, "but she's just the same with tramps and bums of all descriptions. That's why she's sheltering us artists too . . . at least, that's what the village people say."

And by the way, Dr. Sabine was a son of the Bishop who scornfully spoke of a certain New York church as: "The Little Church Around the Corner." And so it has been lovingly called ever since by the actors who worship there. Bishop Sabine's summer home stood next door to Miss Florence's house.

One morning while we were at breakfast, Miss Florence announced the Woodrow Wilsons would arrive at noon, and therefore lunch would be served an hour later than usual. Meanwhile the cats were all about us again. I was getting so fed up with the felines that I began to wonder how we might get rid of them. Presently I caught a thought. Getting up from the table I went to the hardware store and bought a big tin syringe that held a pint of water. On my return I got under the men's table and drove in two nails, so that the syringe could rest there out of sight, but be within easy reach of my chair. Now I felt gay and light-hearted.

At noon while the hungry artists were waiting for Whistling Mary to give the signal, two carriages drove into the back yard, and then we knew that Dr. Woodrow Wilson, Mrs. Wilson, her sister Miss Margaret Axson, and the daughters, Margaret and Jessie, had arrived.

Dr. Wilson was, of course, given a seat at the men's table, and it wasn't long before we not only realized his interest in art, literature and music, but we discovered that he was an excellent story teller. So good indeed that I have long regretted I did not keep a record of them. And in looking back over the years I remember him as a combination of firmness and tolerance, intellect and godliness; a man of affairs yet a scholar, a thinker, yet a doer. And I thoroughly enjoyed his friendship.

No sooner were the Wilson ladies seated at the other table than on came the cats. Presently a kitten, not one of the original sixteen, leaped upon Mrs. Wilson's lap, then with another spring landed upon the table beside her soup plate. While the waitress made a dive for the kitten, I ducked for my tin syringe, charged it from the ice-water pitcher, and then letting drive, I squirted stream after stream in many directions, and drove the bounding cats helter-skelter. I could even hit them on the fly, and those forceful streams of ice-water settled the cat nuisance for many a day.

At first Dr. Wilson seemed out of place at the men's table when he wore his coat. Three days later, however, he discarded it, though he never did unbend enough to roll up his shirtsleeves.

Mrs. Wilson had come to Lyme to study landscape painting under DuMond, the most famous art instructor in North America.

Not only was Miss Florence interested in the work of her guests, but she was forever trying to sell it, and help along the prosperity of her artists. Likewise she was interested in their health, and when she found anyone under the weather, she at once played the nurse or even the doctor. Then one day it happened that I had been feeling unwell for nearly two weeks. My artist friends had recommended this and that, but I couldn't find anything that would fix me up. For two days the dining table had had little attraction for me. As a last resort someone recommended brandy, but Old Lyme was a "local option" town, and there was none to be bought.

Now Dr. Florence took charge of me, and hearing that Henry White was going to motor over the Connecticut River to Saybrook, she scurried to the telephone and asked White to buy her a bottle of brandy. When White returned I was sitting in the drawing-room trying to cheer myself with the company of a number of the men and a half-dozen ladies. Ever since my first appearance that morning I had been feeling very gloomy. My face was unusually long. It seemed as though my chin was almost touching my lap when in comes Dr. Florence with a glass and a bottle of brandy. Her sympathetic black eyes were all aglow with joy, for in this bottle lay the cure. Then she handed me the corkscrew.

"But I don't know how much to take. I've never touched a drop in my life," I said.

"But I don't either," she replied.

"That's all right, Miss Florence," volunteered Metcalf. "I'll pour it out for Arthur."

And he certainly did.

"Now down it straight. That's the boy. It'll make a new man of you before the dinner horn blows."

So up went the glass and down went the grog. Almost immediately my long sad face shortened right up, and broadened into a simple grin—even before I had stopped gasping.

Then I heard Whistling Mary trying to blow the lining out of the dinner horn, and Dr. Florence enquired:

"Will you join us, Arthur?"

"Oh yes, thank you."

I got up to follow the ladies, but when I advanced the door suddenly jumped aside

But strange to say when I got up to follow the ladies, the men were all holding back, and when I advanced to the doorway it suddenly jumped aside. And though I briskly side-stepped too, I now discovered the doorway was trying to avoid me. I tried again, but the darned thing jumped the other way. The ladies, not realizing that the doorway was dodging me, seemed highly amused as they stood and watched me, especially when Hassam and Metcalf held the doorway still, while a couple of the other men helped me through, and escorted me into the dining room. For a sudden rain had driven us there, where we all sat at one long table.

I was now feeling extraordinarily happy and filled with unbelievable gallantry, for I did not want to take my place until I was sure every lady was

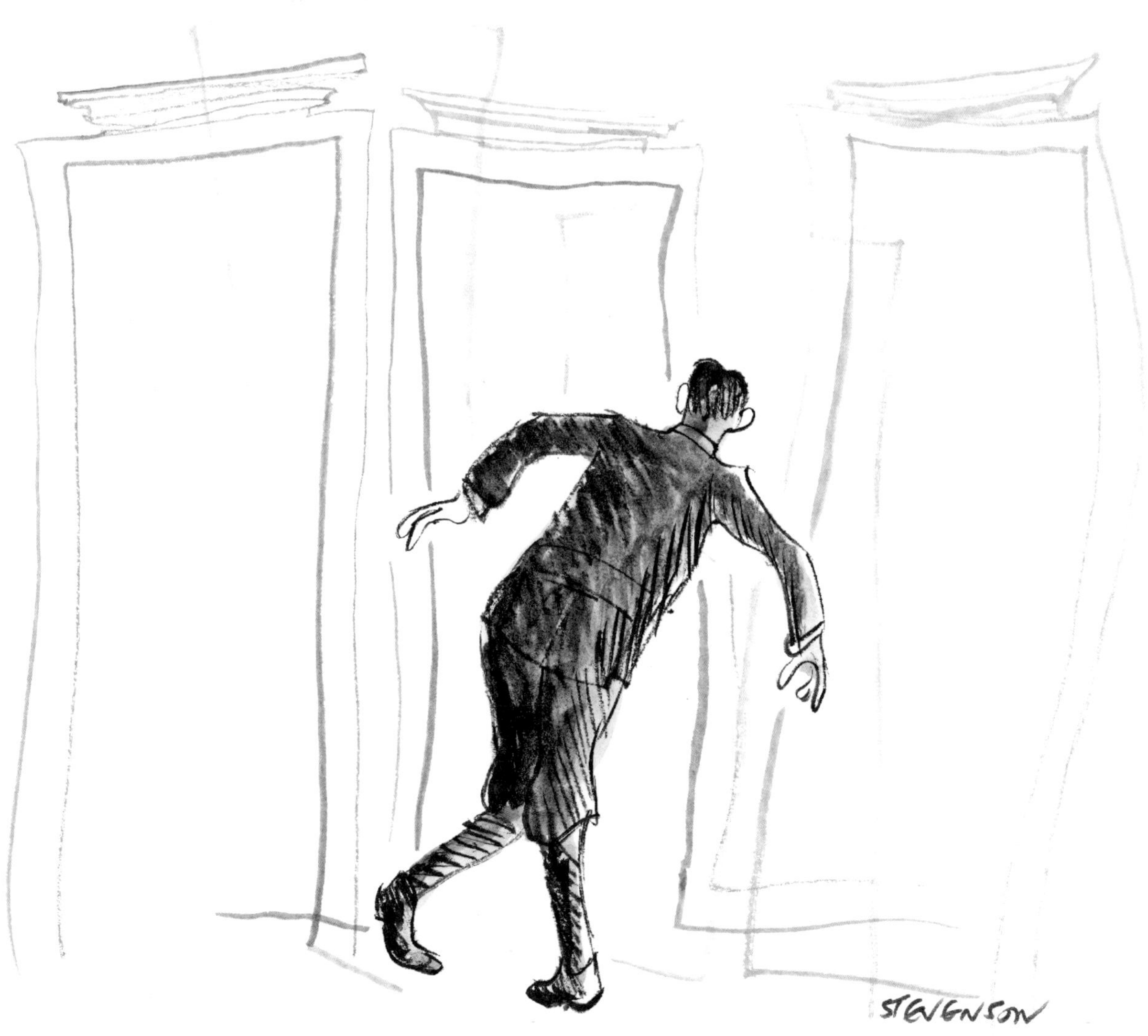

most comfortably seated. Then I regaled the whole company with a series of the funniest stories ever told, for were not the ladies, as well as the men, just laughing fit to kill?

Later, when I happened to glance at my plate, I realized I was delaying the waitresses. They had not only removed my untouched soup, but had now served me with roast beef and boiling hot potatoes. I realized too, that I must at once begin to eat, otherwise they might think I wasn't quite myself . . . the very idea!

With a piece of steaming potato on the tip of my fork, I raised it toward my mouth, but . . . how strange! . . . my mouth wasn't there! And though I tried a number of times to find it, by slyly darting the potato this way and that, I couldn't locate the opening.

And now I found that all my swivels were becoming uncoupled — my elbows, my ankles, my wrists and my knees, but worst of all my neck. That particular swivel was so badly undone that I felt I was going to lose my head. But still the ladies laughed. That made me sore. It would have been quite bad enough if it had been only the men. However, I would show them a thing or two. So I tried again with my fork, but my mouth now jumped about worse than ever. I couldn't get near it. In sheer desperation I made a violent jab and landed the potato in my left ear. I knew it was there because the fork had stabbed me, and the potato was getting hotter and hotter. It became so burning hot that it gave me a new thought . . . Can I be drunk? . . . Yes, I'm drunk! . . . For even the ladies were laughing more than ever! Then I thought of home and mother. What would she think of me? . . . her drunken son!

Instantly a lump that seemed as big as a croquet ball rose and stuck in my throat. I wanted to leave the table. With a great effort I tried to raise my head, but I succeeded in only raising my eyes. And there they stuck, staring up at my eyebrows. Then I felt I was being assisted from my chair, and the last thing I remembered . . . they were unlacing my shoes.

I didn't wake up until nine-thirty next morning. But Dr. Florence, with the assistance of that big, husky, bearded nurse who said: "I'll pour it out for Arthur," had cured me.

And how keen Miss Florence was to entertain her guests, especially in the evenings, and how glad she was when there was something doing. But entertainment was rarely ever planned. It just happened. And perhaps it was all the better for that. She was always ready to accompany a singer upon her piano, or do anything to forward the fun of an evening. Another who generously afforded enjoyment was Harry Hoffman, for what with his tap-dancing, his sleight-of-hand tricks, his playing upon his banjo and flute, his wit and humor, and his laughter-provoking singing, he was an ever ready source of pleasure. But not possessing any such talent, I could seldom make the inmates laugh, except, of course, when they couldn't help laughing at me. Here's an example of the way I occasionally entertained them. I left school at the age of thirteen. The reason I left school so early was that I was fed up with education. I was sick of it. If I proved I could draw pictures, I got thrashed for it. If I proved I couldn't spell, I got thrashed for that too. One winter I was thrashed nearly every morning at a quarter to eleven. That was when the class had returned from recess, and the teacher had had time to examine our dictation slates. I always had from twenty to thirty mistakes. Yet those endless thrashings were all in vain, I was born that way and never in my life was I going to be a good speller. I'm such a bad speller that even dictionaries are of little use, because if one can't spell a word how can one find it in a dictionary? I have eight dictionaries and some of them are so big that it takes a strong man to lift them. But notwithstanding their great size and weight, it's seldom I can ever find in any one of them the word I want.

One night at Lyme, I was working in my studio and I wanted to use the word gnaw, but I wasn't sure I could spell it. I looked through my newest and largest dictionary, but the word was not there, so I looked through it again, just to prove it. For over half an hour I searched in vain, then I got up and went into the house.

Though Miss Florence's famous guests worked hard all day, in the evening they would go on like a lot of kids—even holding spelling bees. At that game Metcalf nearly always won. And when I entered the living room there was Metcalf among many others. There among them too were Woodrow Wilson, Hassam, William Henry Howe, DuMond, Robinson and Edward Rook, all sitting about the fireplace. Mrs. Wilson, Mrs. DuMond, Miss Pope and Bicknell were having a rubber of bridge, and Miss Florence was playing the piano while Hoffman was accompanying her upon his flute. When the duet ended, I cupped my hand and whispered to Metcalf:

"How do you spell 'gnaw'?"

But he looked around in a funny way and asked:

"How do you spell it?"

That irritated me. Fancy, after leaving off my work to come all the way into the house to ask the champion speller of the whole art colony how to spell a word. . . and then he asks me! It made me wild. So I ripped right out loud before the whole crowd:

"I've just bought a new dictionary. I paid seventeen dollars for it. It's about a foot thick. It weighs about fifty pounds. And that great big darn useless thing hasn't got a single 'gnaw' in it!"

But Metcalf didn't look surprised, he merely enquired:

"What did you look under?"

I was getting real mad now, so I growled louder than ever:

"I looked for half an hour under N, and then I looked under K, and there's no such word as 'gnaw' in that great big blasted dictionary!"

And would you believe it? The whole room instantly exploded with laughter. Then on top of that, even while the chairs and sofas were still jiggling, Metcalf had the nerve to ask:

"Arthur . . . when I go back to New York, may I tell that at The Players Club?"

On Saturday Thomas Perkins and his sister Lucy arrived. Tom was a broker in Hartford, and being great friends of one of our artists, Walter Griffin, Tom and Lucy used to come down for weekends, and they always brought a big hamper filled with all sorts of wonderful things for Sunday's breakfast. So it became a regular habit when Tom and Lucy appeared, for Barefoot Mary, Margaret, Whistling Mary and Old Kate to lie in bed on Sunday morning until ten o'clock, and four or five of the artists would get up early to cook breakfast, and serve it too. Each was a specialist in his line, and those breakfasts were well worth remembering. Miss Florence and the ladies enjoyed them greatly.

No matter what new and delicious dishes we offered, Woodrow Wilson always wanted his shredded wheat. So one Sunday morning when it was my turn to wait on table, I selected a nice little bunch of excelsior from a newly arrived packing case, put it in a bowl, poured cream over it, and served it to the future President of the United States. But he didn't detect it until he tried to force it apart with his spoon.

To cut down expenses I was doing my regular weekly washing under the trees

Among the guests that morning was Lewis Cohen. Off and on he had been coming to Miss Florence's house for years and this morning he was handing out presents to his old artist friends in the form of little sketch-boxes. I still have mine. Lewis was a gentleman of unusual generosity and later on was of great help in creating an unforgettable climax to this story.

One Monday morning when I was so hard up that I had to cut down expenses in every way, I was in the middle of doing my regular weekly washing under the trees in the orchard, when Miss Florence, Mrs. Wilson and Mrs. Robinson caught me in the act. On coming back later, when I was in my studio, they went over to my clothes line to inspect my laundry work. Seeing that I had used a pair of Miss Florence's dull scissors to hack off the greater part of the sleeves of my one and only nightshirt, without hemming them, they carried that mutilated garment into the house to put it in order. Later, when a clap of thunder reminded me to rush out and take in my washing, I discovered that my old nightshirt now looked as though I had stolen it from some bride's trousseau. They had sewn to each of those six-inch sleeves a four-inch flounce of gorgeous lace.

Now it looked exactly as though it needed a chaperon. So I never got in bed with it, but just gently folded it up, and placed it nice and handy . . . in case of fire.

When Lyme's annual art exhibition had been open several days and no pictures had been sold, the artists were looking rather glum. The sales management was in charge of a number of women chosen from Lyme's elite, but its weak point was that all those ladies might be present one hour, and the next hour none. It was just such a day, when a good crowd had come from New York, Boston and even Chicago, that I happened in. But as no sales were being made, I stepped up and sold five sketches by

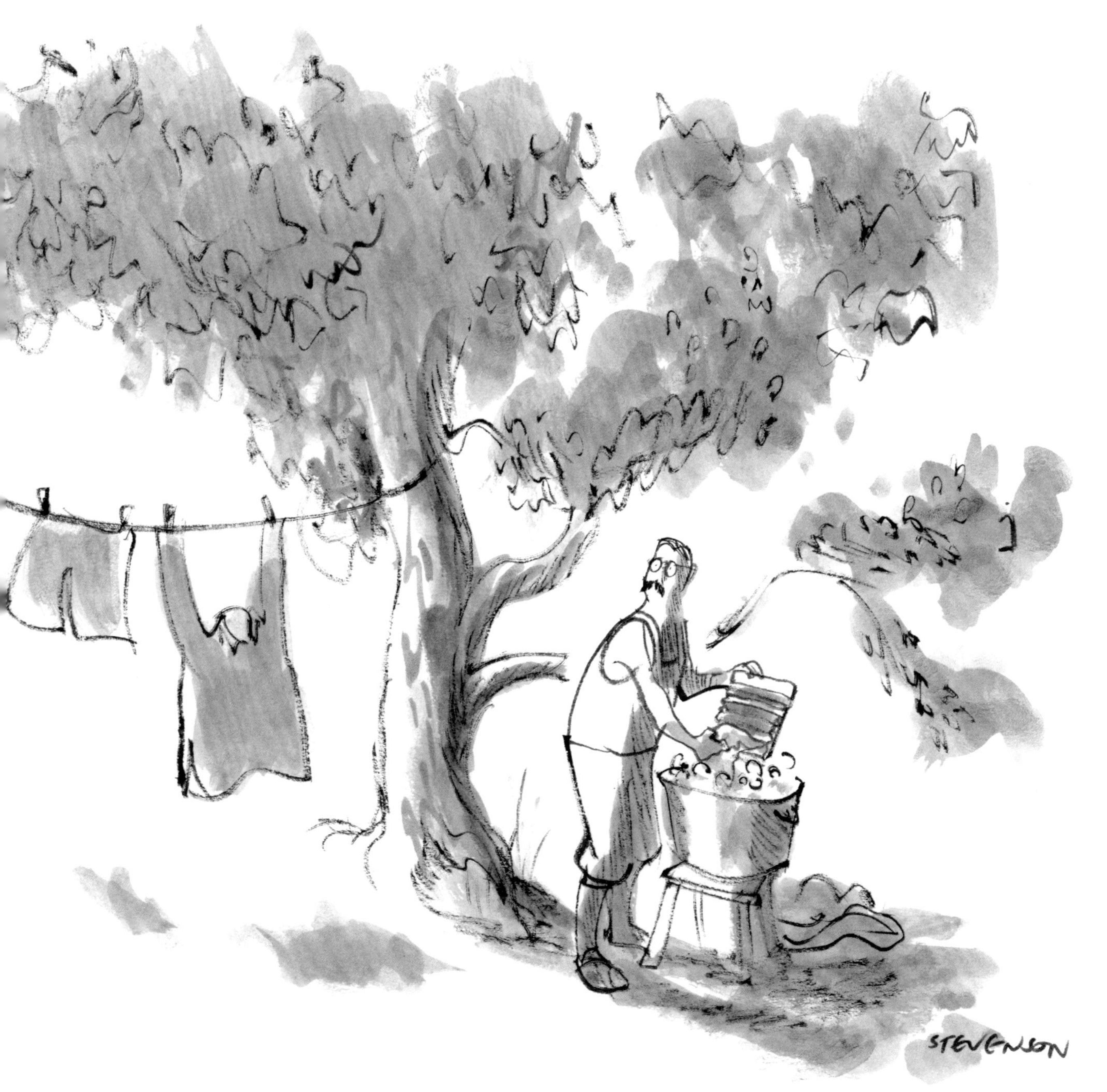
STEVENSON

other artists within an hour. When the management heard about it, they
asked me to take charge. I said I would if I could choose two assistants.
Then with Miss Florence and Mrs. Woodrow Wilson to help, we put our
heads together and decided that they should try to separate the wives from
their husbands. Because, as the ladies explained, wealthy women never
want paintings, they want new dresses, new jewelry, new furs and new
motor cars. I soon saw that they were right and their wisdom soon brought
results. It was amusing too when a husband would excitedly whisper:

"Quick, here comes my wife. Slap a sold ticket on it, then she can't say
a word."

But my two assistants soon tired of the wives, and suggested that I tackle
them, while they had a turn with the husbands. Then for the first time in
my life I did a proper job at flirting, just to help the cause along, and the
show closed with a lot of sales to our credit.

However, even with that good luck some of the artists still left without
making a single sale. But that was nothing new, for often the best work is
overlooked until the artist is dead and buried.

Metcalf was among the unlucky number, and several weeks later he
called me into his studio to show me his most recent painting.

It was a beautiful moonlight conception of Miss Florence's house.
The moonlit sky, the sombre shadows of the projecting roof, the four Ionic
pillars, the glow of lamplight from the lower windows and the open
doorway ready to receive Miss Florence as she came up the stone walk.
It was called: "May Night."

Presently there was a rap at the studio door and in came Miss Florence.

"Oh, how heavenly!" she exclaimed. "Oh, Mr. Metcalf, it's perfectly
beautiful!"

"It's yours, Miss Florence," Metcalf said.

"Nonsense, man, you're dreaming!"

"No, I'm not. I painted it for you."

"Don't be foolish . . . it'll sell for thousands!"

"But it's the only way I can pay for my board."

"I won't take it. It's the best thing you've ever done. When you show it in New York, they'll snap it up at once, and everything will be lovely."

By refusing to accept that painting Miss Florence created the turning point in Metcalf's career. For when "May Night" was shown the following winter at the Corcoran Art Gallery in Washington, it not only won the Clark gold medal, but it was awarded the first cash prize and the painting was bought by the Gallery. His success soared from that time on and he died wealthy.

But having lived ten years in Miss Florence's house, frequently sharing her confidence, and often helping her with her business affairs, I take pleasure in stating that I have yet to learn of any artist guest who ever became a financial loss to her. As a hostess she was a remarkable success, but as a businesswoman she was a failure. Yet her charm as hostess made her the greatest benefactor Lyme ever possessed. It was she who raised the price of farms and of village lots, caused the renovating of old houses and the building of many a new one, made the merchants well-to-do, and brought prosperity to the whole region . . . but not to herself.

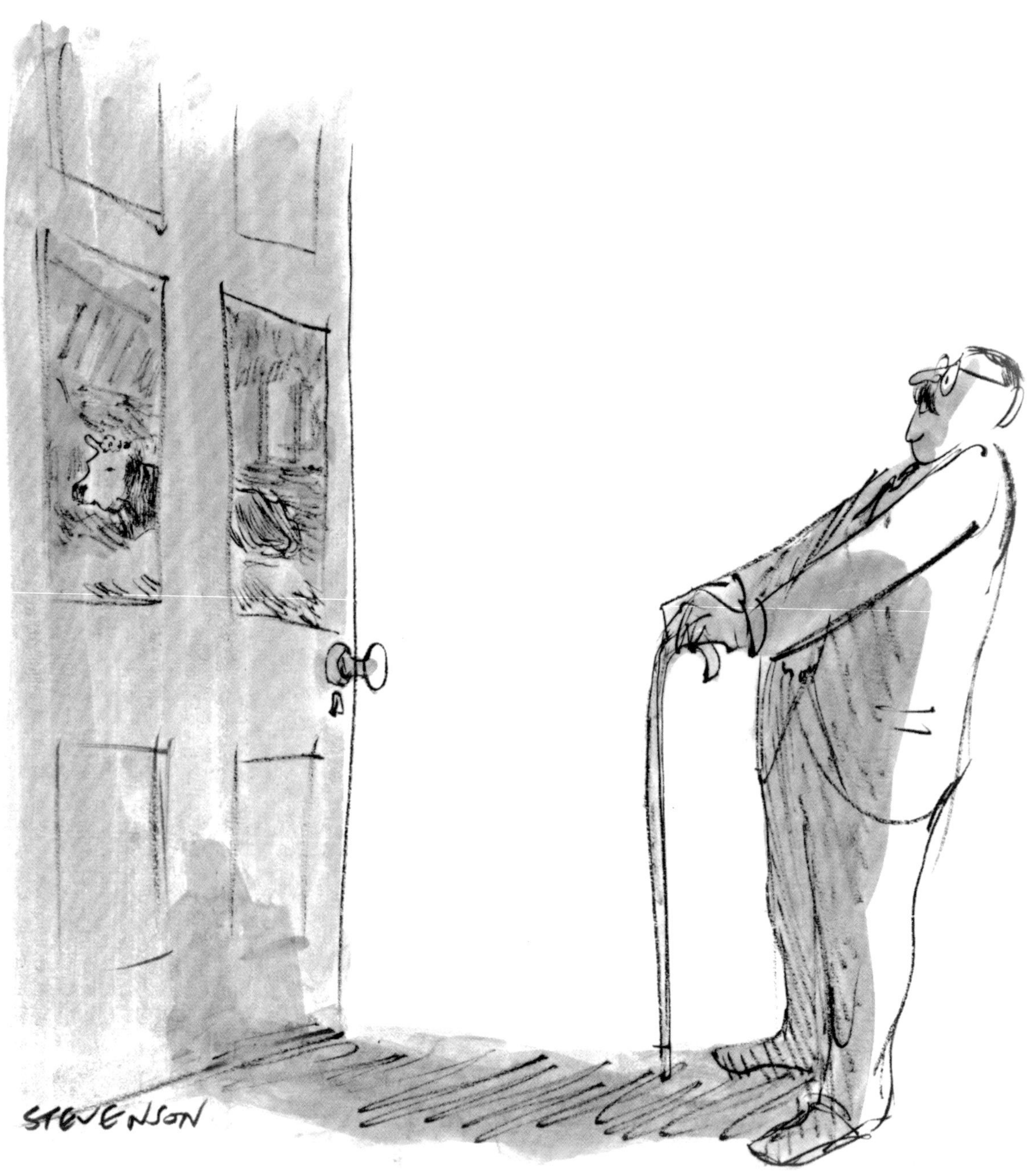
Stevenson

*A Mr. Wilson from Chicago wanted to
buy first the painting on the door panels —
then the door — and finally the house*

Now winter was approaching, their happiest season was over, for business
reasons the painters had to return to New York. Now how empty and
forlorn and tattered and worn was that beautiful old home.

Once again Miss Florence was utterly depressed with financial worry,
and it was telling upon her health. Several times she had had to take to
her bed.

Then it happened one gloomy afternoon when she was having a lonely
cup of tea in her drawing room, that a stranger was announced.

He was a well-known picture collector from Chicago, a Mr. Wilson,
whose first name I've forgotten. He came to see the famous panels, and
while Miss Florence was showing him over the house, he took a great fancy
to the William Henry Howe panels on one of the drawing-room doors.
Suddenly he asked:

"Miss Griswold, how much do you want for the door?"

"Oh, Mr. Wilson, I've never dreamed of setting a price on any of
the panels."

He, however, was determined to buy and started to make bids. Higher
and higher he went until Miss Florence felt she really ought to sell, on
account of being so much in debt, but as it was a present from Howe she
felt she should not part with it, without his consent. At last Wilson said:

"I'll tell you what I'll do, Miss Griswold, I'll either take the door as it
stands and replace it with a new one, or I'll have the panels removed and
put in others.

"I'll give you eighteen hundred dollars for the door."

"Oh no, Mr. Wilson, I really can't sell it . . . the door is part of the house."

"Well that's all right, I'll buy the house. How much do you want for it?"

Flooded with thoughts of her present troubles, and flooded too with memories of her girlhood days, when she played upon her golden harp and tuned it to romance, Miss Florence pondered dreamily a while, and then innocently and absent-mindedly replied:

"No, no, Mr. Wilson, I mustn't think of it, not for a single moment . . . for you know I've always counted on the house going with me."

"Holy smoke! Miss Griswold . . . I can't go any further. I'm a married man!"

How she laughed that evening when she told us that story! But months later when old Uncle Howe heard of it, he swore like a trooper, and wanted to know:

"Why in hell didn't she sell it? I'd have gladly painted her half-a-dozen more!"

But that was just Miss Florence all over again and she never would, or could, change.

The nearer winter came the harder some of the merchants pressed her to pay, and worry knocked her out again and kept her in bed for days. Something had to be done, and that very soon, or she would be overtaken with a complete breakdown. She needed a change. A happy holiday. Several of her wealthy friends, both in New York and elsewhere, had coaxed her to visit them, but she always refused, believing she ought to stay at home to attend to business.

At last I devised a plan. I wrote a number of letters to those friends, told them of her ill health, her financial troubles, and how necessary it was for her to get away on a holiday. I asked them to invite her again, but not to mention my name. A few days later when the replies came, Miss Florence exclaimed: "How strange! And how nice too! Here are five invitations from old friends who want me to visit them, and they all came today! Goodness, how I would love to go. But I'll have to stay and look after business."

"Look after business! Honestly, Miss Florence, you make me laugh. Staying to look after business with only two boarders in the house. That's no excuse whatever. You must go at once.

"Your health, your happiness and your next summer's business depend on your going now. Old Kate can act as cook and chaperon, Margaret can be housekeeper and maid, and Harry and I can be your business managers to collect board money from chance guests and chase the bill collectors away. Now's the time for you to go, and I won't listen to no. If you don't write and accept those invitations, I'm going to do it for you."

Ten days later it came about that Old James and I drove her down to the station and helped her aboard the train. That evening I received a telegram from Chapin of Scribner's. He wanted to see me about making some illustrations. So I left for New York in the morning. After finishing my business, I called upon some of my Lyme artist friends, among them Lewis Cohen. While he was showing me over his studio apartment on West Sixty-Seventh Street, Lewis remarked:

"Art, I've bought a cottage in Lyme. So I won't be with Miss Florence any more, and I want to make her a suitable present for all her kindness to me, but I can't think of the right thing. Can you help me out?"

Instantly my thoughts flashed back to her old home. What would give her the greatest pleasure? What would be the kindest thing one might do for her? In a moment I replied:

"The finest thing you could do would be to make a start at fixing up her home. That's been her lifelong dream. Why not help make it come true? Think of her awful drawing-room. Think of its cracked and broken ceiling, its stained and peeling wallpaper, its crumpled and torn window shades, its cracked and worn paintwork, its broken window cords and shattered window panes, its busted furniture. Think what it would mean to her if some fairy godmother waved a wand, and restored only that one room to all its former charm and beauty. Lewis, tackle the drawing-room. That will give her more pleasure than anything else you can do."

"Excellent! . . . splendid! . . . you're a brick, you old redheaded beggar! I'll do it!" laughed Lewis Cohen.

"Art, when you go back to Lyme get an estimate on having the drawing-room ceiling fixed and tinted, the room papered, the woodwork painted, the windows fixed. And skip over to New London, and make a dicker with some good cabinet maker to send men to overhaul and recover the furniture. I'll select the wallpaper and furniture coverings here, and ship them up to you."

Furthermore, we agreed not to let Miss Florence know any thing about it, and that I was to try to keep her away until it was finished, so that it would be a surprise for her.

As I knew Lewis had a private income, I did not worry about the cost of his gift, and when sending him a list of the drawingroom furniture, I included the furniture in the halls, so that he "would have plenty of articles from which to make a choice." He replied:

"That's a good idea about the furniture in the halls. And send me the sizes of the walls, and I'll buy paper for the halls too."

In a few days the paper and coverings arrived, and the men started to work.

One day Mrs. Pope dropped in for lunch. She came to inspect the work on the new house for Harry and Beatrice. And, of course, I had to explain the great secret, and what a surprise it was going to be to Miss Florence.

"But Arthur, how about the stair carpet?"

"Mrs. Pope, there were holes in it big enough to stick my head through. We can't put it down again."

"I wish you'd measure the stairs and the floors of both halls too, and give me a sample of the wallpaper, so I can buy carpet to match."

In less than a week big rolls of carpet arrived all ready to put down.

Things began to hum: carpenters, masons, well diggers, house painters, paper hangers, cement workers, others

That night as I lay in bed I did some thinking. It was a bully story as far as it had gone, but that wasn't far enough. It ought to go right through to a bang-up finish. Then I chuckled when I realized that I wasn't writing this story, I was living it. That was all the more reason it should have a good climax. And I had better get busy.

The next day I wrote over twenty letters to the old crowd, about the great surprise Lewis Cohen and Mrs. Pope were going to have for Miss Florence, and that it was to be kept a secret. In a few days the replies were all in and everyone volunteered to help. Mrs. Woodrow Wilson wrote to say the Doctor and she would be glad if I would kindly have two of the largest bedrooms redecorated from ceilings to floors, and new shades and curtains for the windows, and please send the bills to her. The artists responded splendidly too. Bicknell wrote to say if I could inveigle some rich person to buy coverings for some of the bedroom furniture, Robinson and he would run up and do the recovering. For both of them were excellent craftsmen. So I just happened to show that letter to a certain rich lady, and when she handed it back to me, she smiled:

"I'm inveigled, but you mustn't mention my name."

Then when everything was going full swing who should drop in but Tom Perkins, the broker from Hartford. He was motoring to Boston and had stopped for lunch. When he found "Miss Florence away and the artists just ripping the insides out of her house," as the village people said, I had to explain.

"Art, I've got to be in on this! Not only because Lucy and I have spent some of our happiest weekends here, but because Miss Florence has been responsible for bringing together many distinguished painters and men of affairs, and in that way has turned an old poverty-stricken village into a prosperous and famous community. That's why I want to give her a hand.

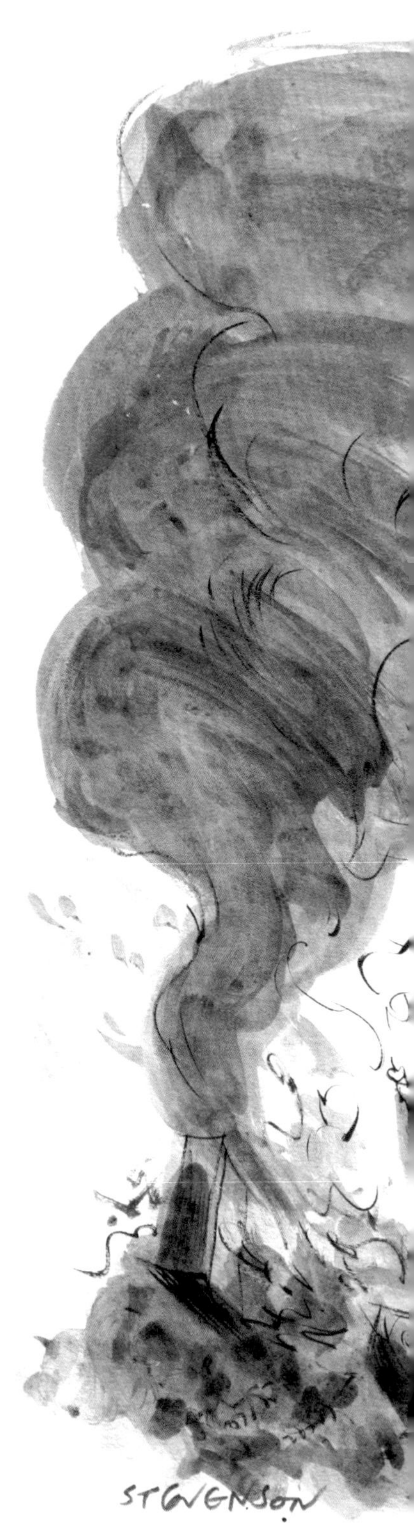

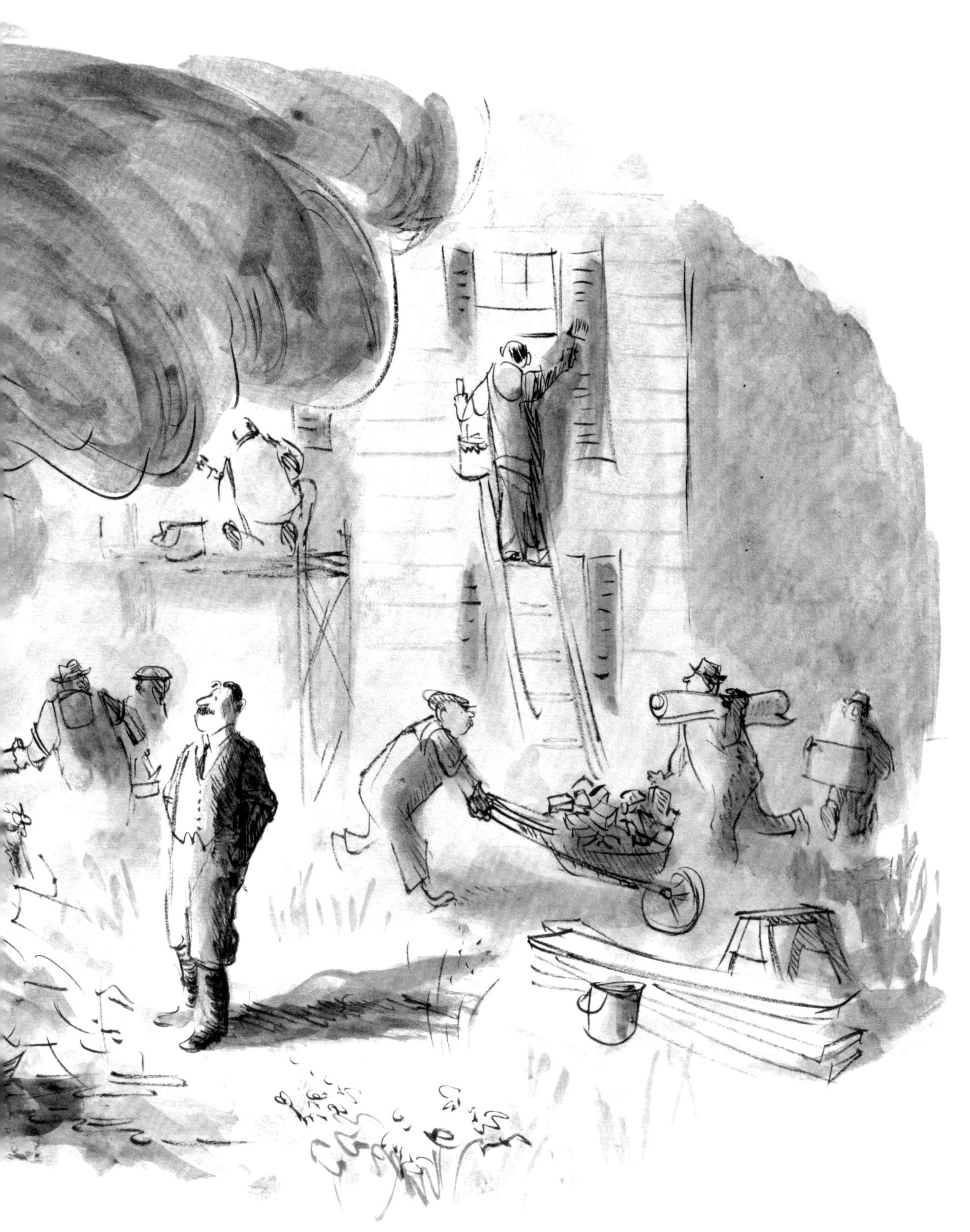

And I want to do the things that ought to be done to save the old house."

Now things certainly did begin to hum. I promised Tom I would act as foreman of the job. Then for over six weeks I never did a tap of my own work, but was kept busy looking after the twenty-eight workmen on the place: carpenters, masons, plumbers, well-diggers, housepainters, drain-diggers, paper-hangers, cement workers and others.

"Margaret, you've always wanted to get rid of all the useless junk that clutters this house, so go to it now. I'll start a bonfire in the back yard, and what we ought to save, we can put in the attic or the hayloft. And Margaret, how many cats are there now?"

"Eighteen, Mr. Heming."

"There'll be a lot less when Miss Florence comes home."

Now for several months things just hummed along, but what a time we had keeping "the patron saint" away—as *The New York Times* called her. And strange to say there were only two cats now left to welcome her, Toto and Padjkins, her favorites.[2]

But at last we could keep her away no longer. She was coming home today. So Lyme's Civil War Veteran, General Perkins, came up to the house to see its transformation. He was one of Miss Florence's oldest friends. He had known her since she was a child. And when he stood in the hall, and looked into the drawing-room, he threw up his arms and yelled:

"My God, Heming! Where did you put it all!"

That proved what splendid work Margaret had done in supplying me with enough junk to keep my bonfire burning for eight days. Old James had done fine work too. His present to Miss Florence was a number of rustic cedar seats and arbors that he had made for her lawn.

Another person who did Miss Florence a great kindness was the local judge, Joseph S. Huntington, but his gift was not in relation to fixing up the house. That morning Joe had called upon some of the merchants and handed them little slips of paper, and they in return had given him larger ones upon which they had written their signatures. Then Joe had sneaked in Miss Florence's side door when no one was looking, tiptoed up the back

2 *Although Heming's typescript gives the cat's name as Ioto, this is presumably a typo as Willard Metcalf referred to the cat as Toto in three letters to Florence Griswold. See Willard Metcalf to Florence Griswold, November 29, 1905. Willard Leroy Metcalf Papers, Archives of American Art; Willard Metcalf to Florence Griswold, December 11 and December 15, 1905. Florence Griswold Papers, Lyme Historical Society Archives, Florence Griswold Museum.*

stairs to her bedroom, and spread out upon her bed those little papers that represented paid bills that totalled over eight hundred dollars.

Then, not knowing about it, I happened to meet Joe as he came out of that side door, and he hit me such a welt on my left leg, with his little bamboo cane, that I winced with pain. No doubt he just did that because he was feeling so happy. But when I swung round to give him a proper cussing, I saw that he was now swinging nothing but the handle of his broken stick, and it made me burst out laughing.

But what Tom Perkins had done was far more wonderful. He had spent thousands of dollars upon the house. The exact amount I cannot say, for none but the Lord and Tom ever knew; but I'll bet it kept St. Peter busy every night keeping track of Tom's record.

Here's a complete list of what was already done, and what was still underway, when Miss Florence came home that day:

The roof was re-shingled, the chimneys mended, the front porch's pillars, floor and steps restored, all the shutters fixed, the windows put in order, the whole outside of the house given two coats of paint, two new bedrooms with hot and cold water put in, a new well dug, a cement engine house built for a gasoline engine to pump water into the big tank placed in the house, and a sewer dug down to the river; a hotel cooking range put in the kitchen, the halls and drawing-room and the principal bedrooms redecorated and most of the furniture mended and recovered. Besides there were many gifts such as rugs and carpets for the stairs, halls and other rooms, as well as window decorations, to say nothing of the flowers that were there to greet her.

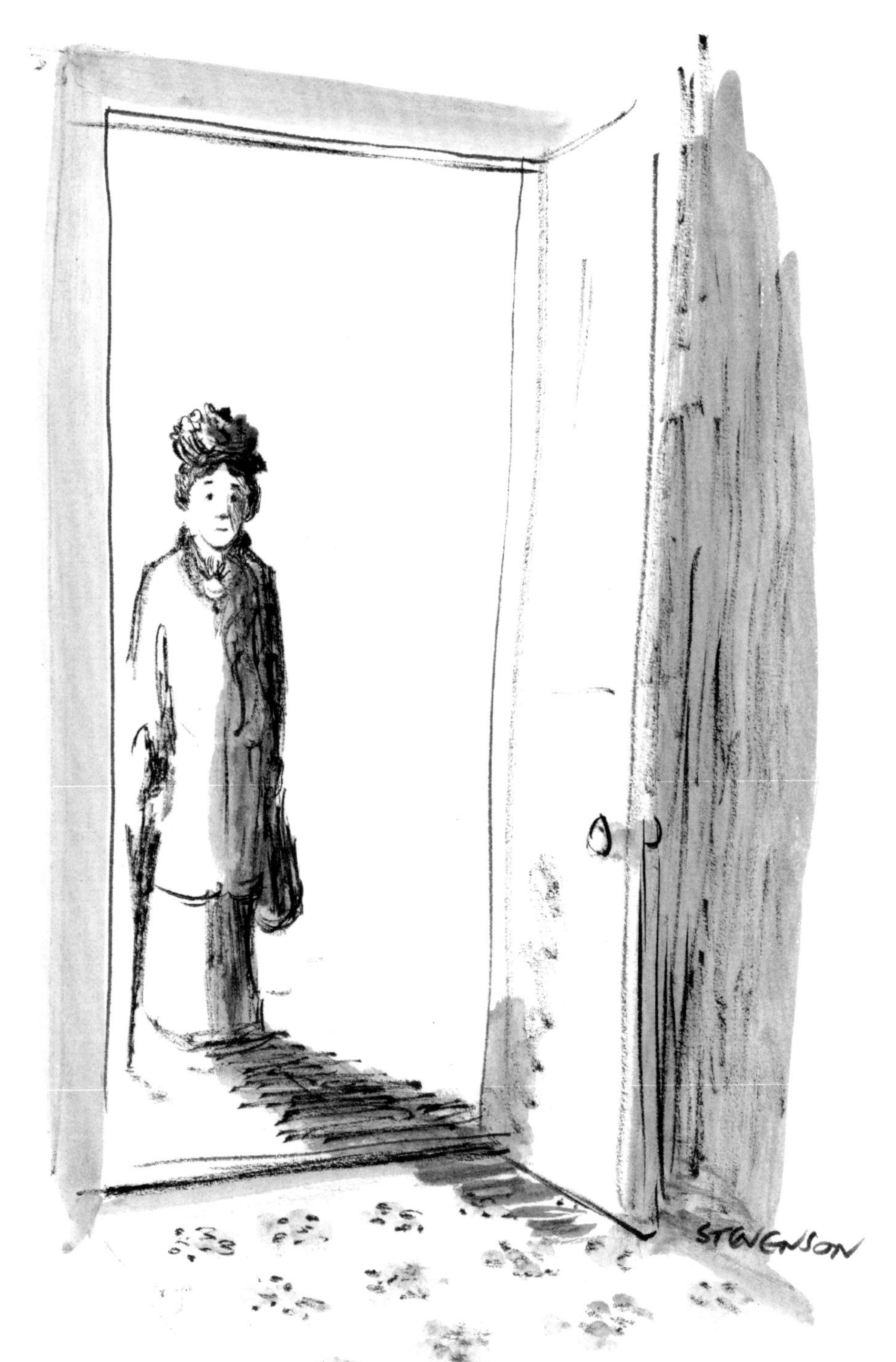

And how many willing hands had helped Harry and me in the final arrangements. The worst of the fly-specked engravings had gone to the attic, the best to the bedrooms, and the fine paintings that had been given her were now properly hung. Everything was in order. What a splendid transformation had taken place. The house now looked beautiful, far more beautiful than she had ever seen it before.

At the luncheon table Mrs. Robinson said:

"Only one person should remain here to receive Miss Florence this afternoon, and that person should be 'Old Uncle Art.'"

So I had to stay, while some went calling, others went painting, and the servants all went out in Judge Huntington's canoe—but the Judge didn't know it. Then I went all over the house and closed every door, so that she could only see one room at a time. And it was arranged that Sterling's livery rig should bring her home from the train. On the way up it rained, so the driver pulled down the side curtains of the carriage, thus when it came up the lane and into the back yard, Miss Florence didn't notice the outside transformation of her handsome old home.

I went out to greet her. She looked tired and forlorn. Evidently she was already worrying over those unpaid bills—but think of Joe's surprise for her. When I opened the big back door of the main hallway and she stepped in, she began to tremble as she saw how lovely it looked with its new wallpaper, its new carpet, and its new coverings on all the furniture. But she didn't speak. She just went on ahead of me and opened the drawing-room door. And there she stood gazing for several moments—perhaps because she hadn't strength to enter. Then at last she tried to reach that lovely old chair that stood beside the center table—the one that formerly had a pile of books beneath it so the guests wouldn't hit the floor. But now it was all ready and waiting to take her in its big comfortable arms, and as she crumpled up into it her arms and head went down upon the table and she began to sob as though her heart would break.

Instantly I wheeled round, and went up two flights of stairs, three steps at a time, for though I've never run from bears or wolves or wildcats, I always have to light out when a woman weeps.

About fifteen minutes later, as I sat in my bedroom, I heard her moving about below. She was opening door after door. Then at least I heard the upper stairs creaking. She was coming up to my room, but very slowly, as though she hardly had strength enough to move. Finally she stood in my open doorway. She looked very weak from weeping. Her eyes were very red. Her face was tear stained, and tears were still falling. Then, in little more than a whisper, she almost breathlessly exclaimed:

"Oh Arthur . . . I never knew I had such wonderful friends . . . It's a dream of a lifetime come true!"

That was in the early spring of 1910, and just as Woodrow Wilson said: "The memory of those carefree days in Lyme is still very fresh with me, and very fragrant."

ABOUT THE AUTHORS

Arthur Heming, the distinguished Canadian painter, illustrator, and writer, was born in 1870 in Paris, Ontario, one of eleven children. He attended the

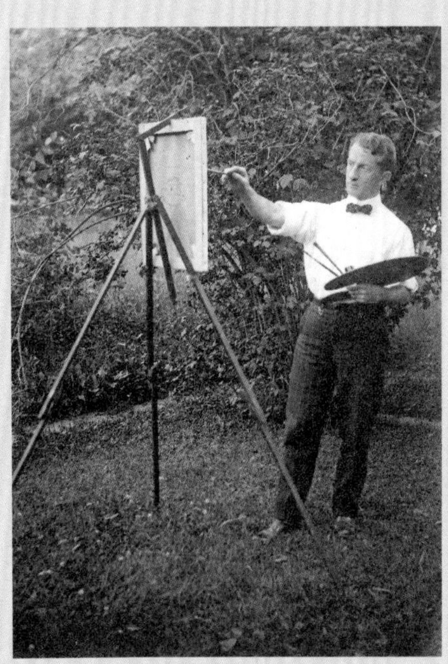

Hamilton Art School in Canada and taught there from 1887 to 1890. He then left to study in New York at the Art Students League and was a pupil of Frank Vincent DuMond. He also studied with Frank Brangwyn in 1904. He was an excellent athlete which prepared him for his travels of thousands of miles in the wilderness. He traveled the Artic Circle for *Harper's Magazine* as an illustrator and wrote and illustrated several books. Among these was *Spirit Lake*, a story of the Hudson's Bay Company, and *The Drama of the Forests*. In the great northland he came into personal contact with the native hunters and wildlife of Canada, and his work is not only genuine art but also an authentic record of historical value. Arthur Heming came to Lyme in 1902 as a student of Frank Vincent DuMond and was therefore one of the first members of the Old Lyme Art Colony who lived at the Florence Griswold House. He died in 1940. His work is represented in a number of galleries in Canada including the Canadian National Gallery and the Royal Ontario Museum.

The acclaimed illustrator **James Stevenson** worked for over thirty years at *The New Yorker*, producing 2,000 cartoons, 80 covers, as well as reporting and fiction. From 2003 to 2011, he wrote and illustrated the popular op-ed column "Lost and Found New York," about historic sites and people, for *The New York Times*. Stevenson is the author or illustrator of over 100 books for children and his work for *The New Yorker* and *The New York Times* has been reprinted in book form.

The Painted Panels of
the Florence Griswold House

Beginning in 1900, members of the Old Lyme Art Colony began to
decorate selected door and wall panels on the first floor of Florence
Griswold's boardinghouse, first in the front hallway and parlor and then
in the dining room at the rear of the house. During the next several
decades, these artists completed over forty paintings in the house,
including Henry Rankin Poore's *The Fox Chase*, a caricature of colony
members that appears on the opening pages of this book. The color plates
in this section depict the remainder of the panels, first those on each of
the four walls of the dining room and then those on door panels
elsewhere on the first floor.

Inspired by decorations he had seen at European country inns, colony
founder Henry Ward Ranger initiated the tradition of painting door
panels with *Bow Bridge by Moonlight*. Henry Rankin Poore adorned the
door's other panel with a nocturnal landscape depicting a dog baying
at Ranger's moon. Four artists painted eight more door panels in the
Griswold House. Some were entirely new compositions; others derived
from paintings for which the artists were already well known.

Before 1906, Childe Hassam and other artists painted doors in the
dining room to complement those elsewhere on the first floor of the
Griswold House. That year, artist Willard Metcalf suggested adding
painted wooden panels to the dining room walls, the center of the art
colony's social life, as a tribute to Florence Griswold. In all, the room
contains thirty-eight paintings by thirty-three artists depicting subjects that
range from the Old Lyme countryside to such far-flung locales as Europe,
the Canadian wilderness, and the Far East. As a gallery of works by the
colony's "comrades of the brush," the dining room acquired considerable
fame. "Every stranger within the gates of Lyme wants to see it—and to
see it is to admire it," remarked one journalist in 1914.

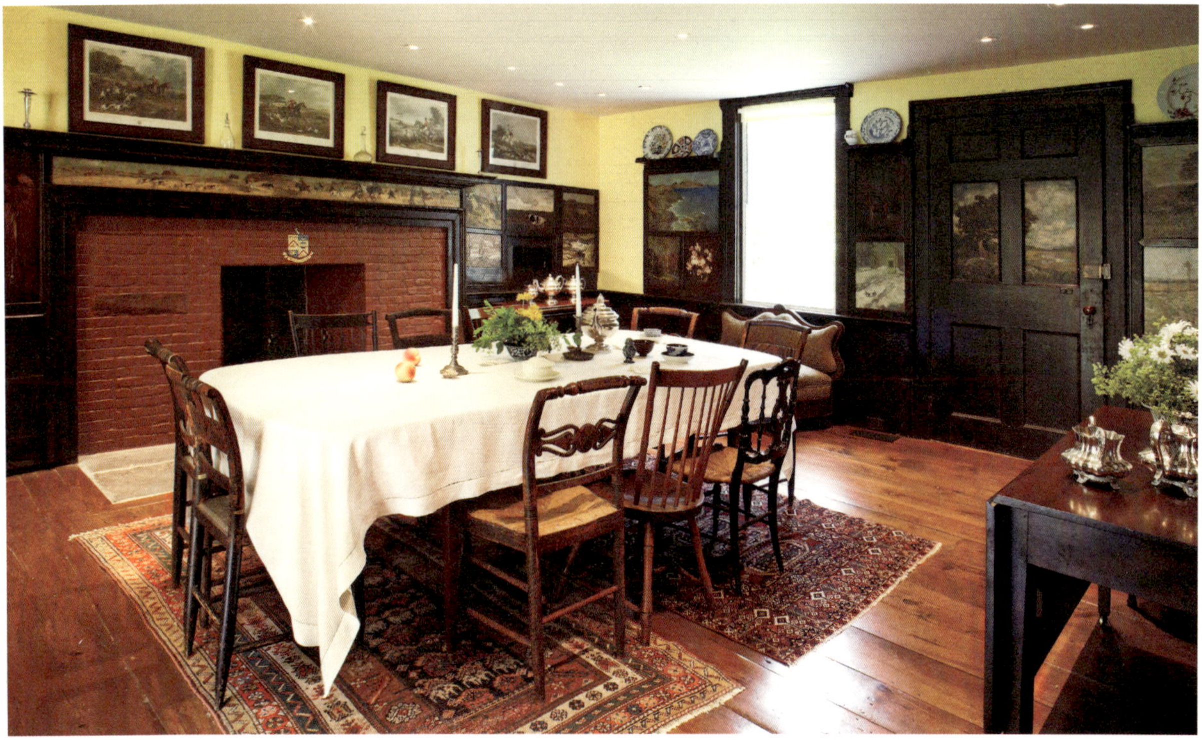

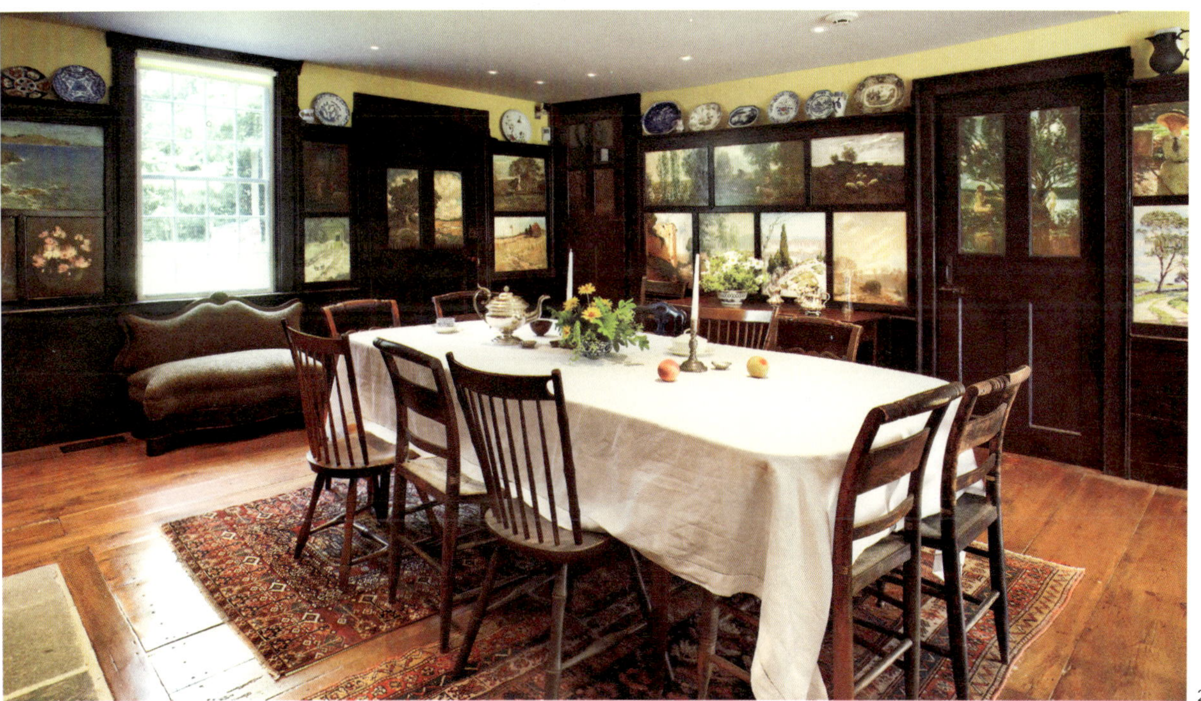

1 Wall and door panels on the west and north walls of the Florence Griswold
dining room, with the *Fox Chase* frieze over the fireplace.
2 North and east walls of the dining room.

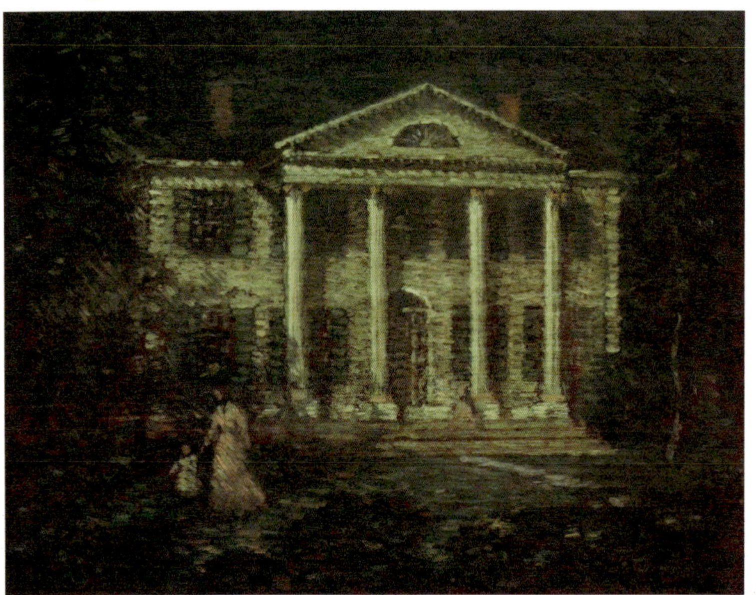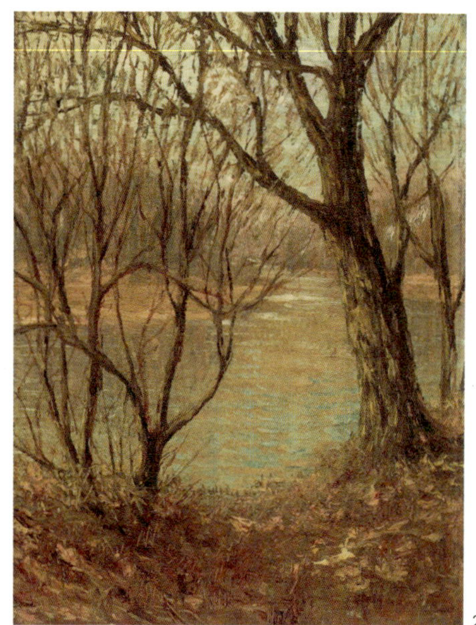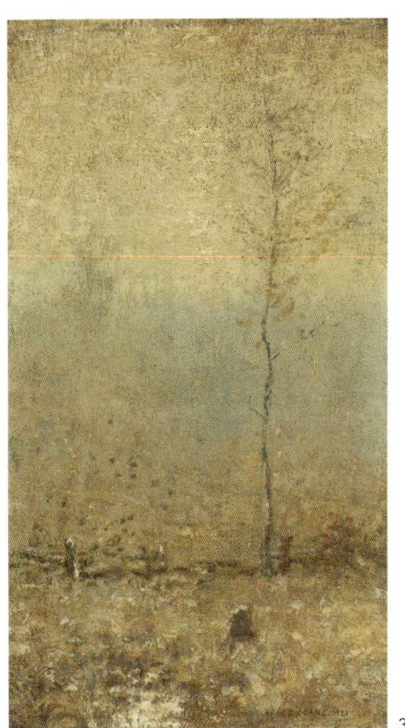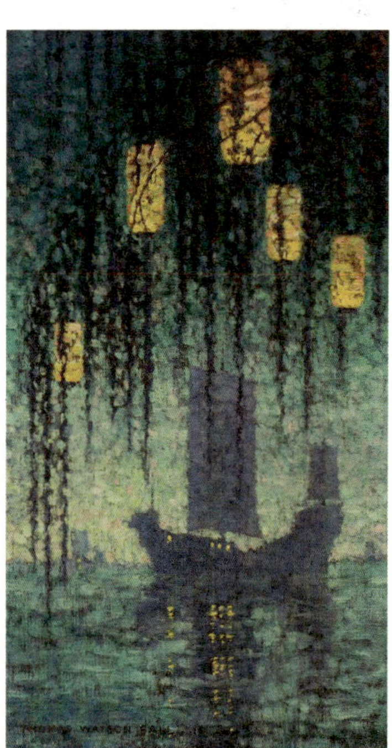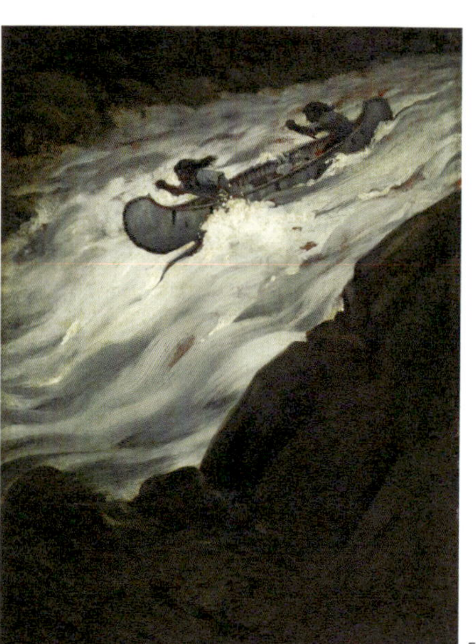

1 *Florence Griswold House by Moonlight*, 1905, Will Howe Foote

2 *By the River*, 1907, Harry Hoffman

3 *December Morn*, 1921, Bruce Crane

4 *Chinese Twilight*, Thomas Watson Ball

5 *Shooting Death's Rapids*, 1906, Arthur Heming

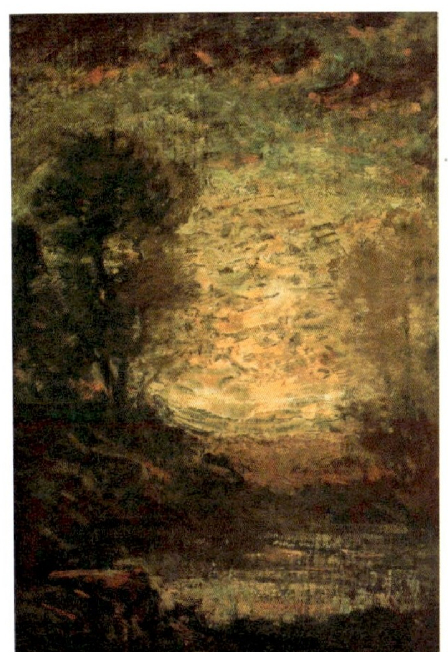
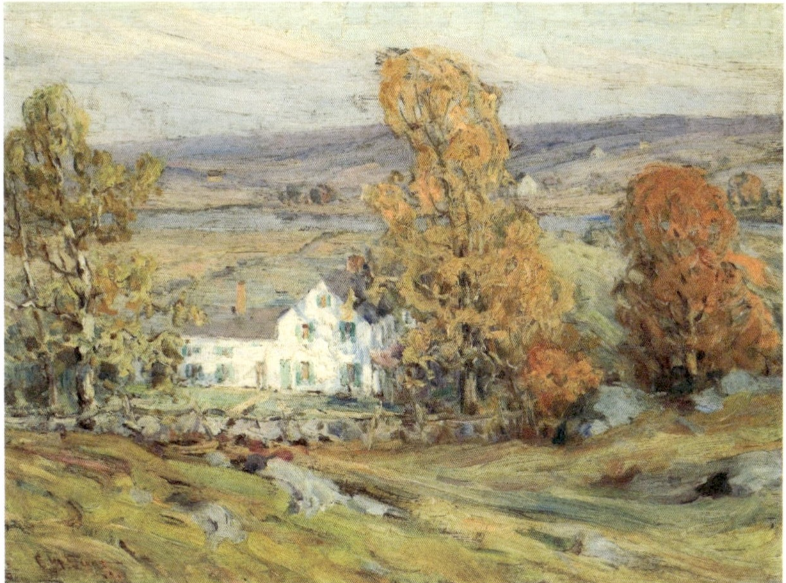
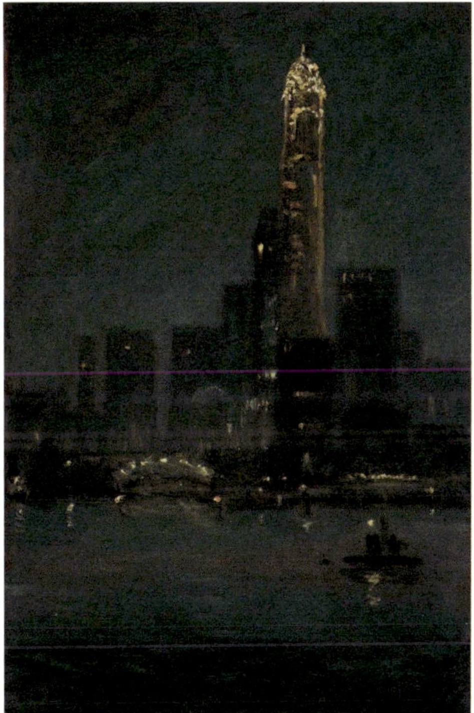

6 *Sunset Glow*, Gustave Wiegand
7 *Autumn*, 1907, Charles Morris Young
8 *The Singer Building at Night*, ca. 1908–10, Charles Vezin
9 *Venetian Fancy*, ca. 1905–06, Robert Nisbet

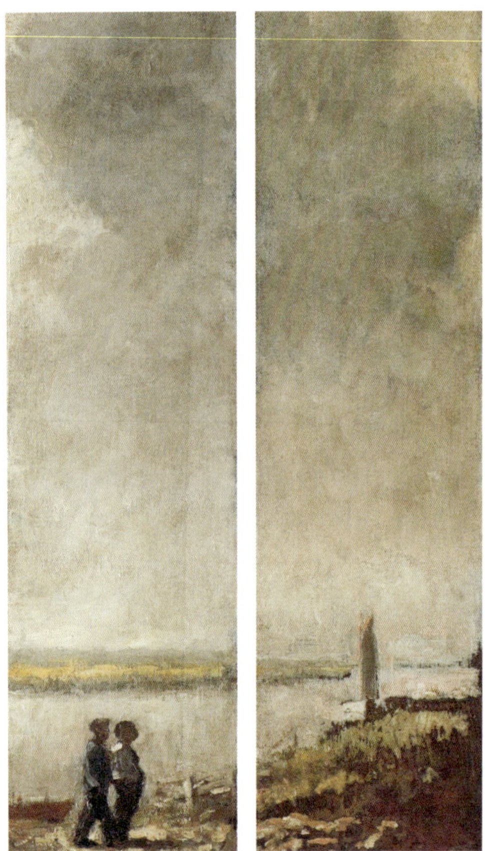

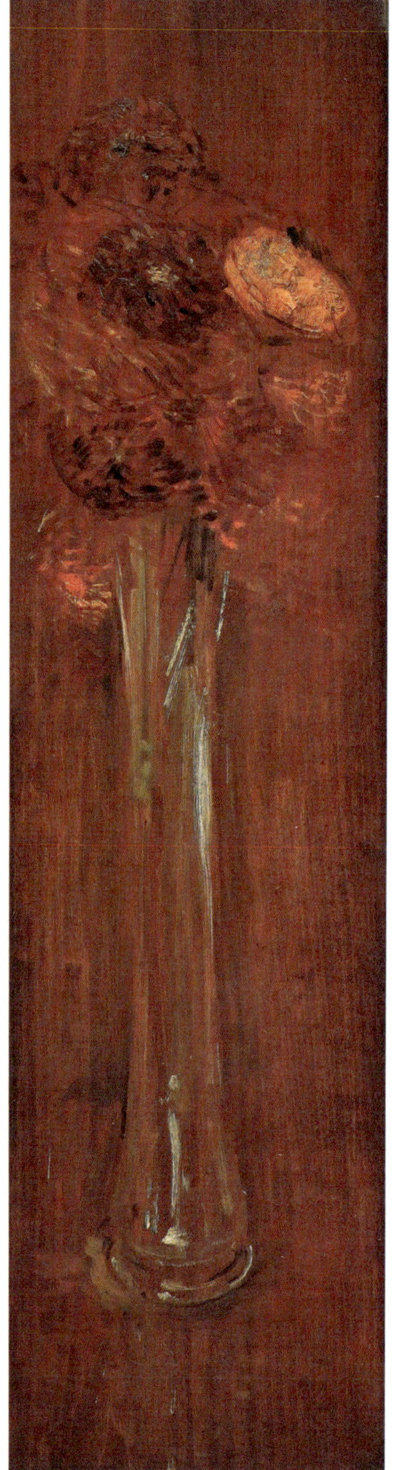

1 *Summer Scene,* ca. 1905–06, Gifford Beal
2 *Dahlia Study,* Childe Hassam

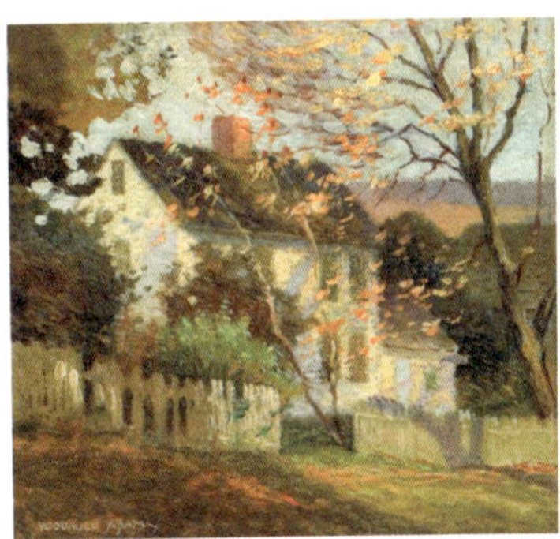
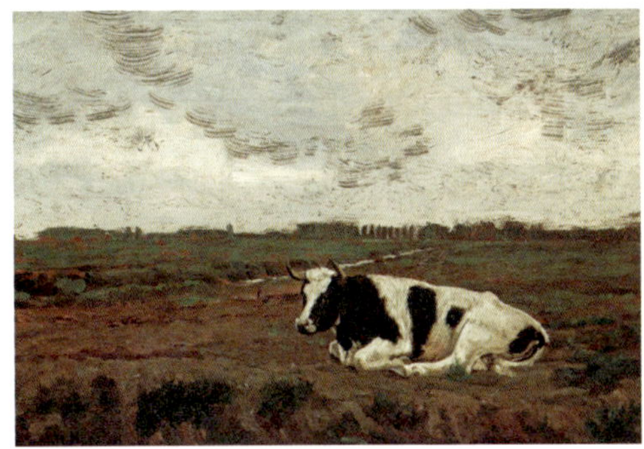
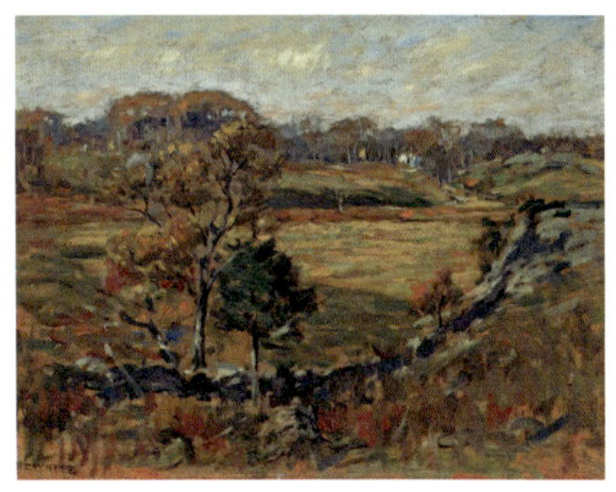
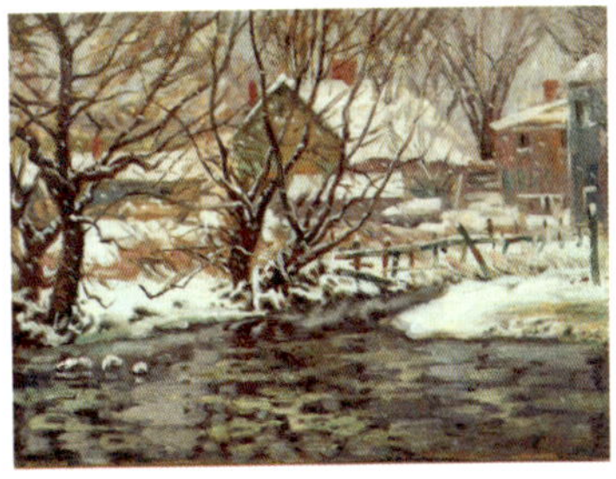
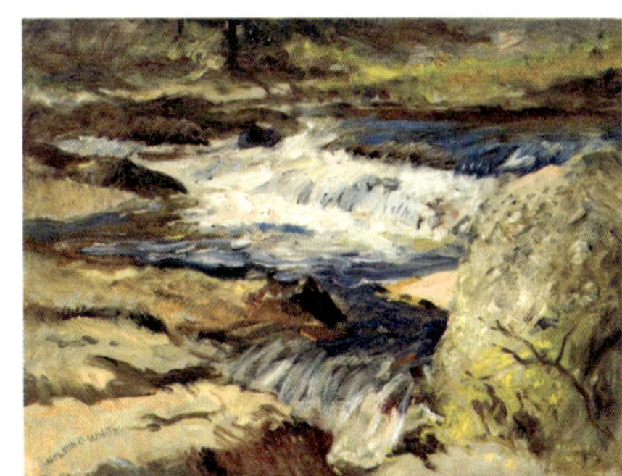

3 *White Cottage in Autumn*, Woodhull Adams

4 *Cattle Near Schiedam, Holland*, 1906, George Glenn Newell

5 *Autumn Landscape*, ca. 1904, Henry C. White

6 *Ipswich in Winter*, 1908, Henry R. Kenyon

7 *Stream and Rapids*, Nelson C. White

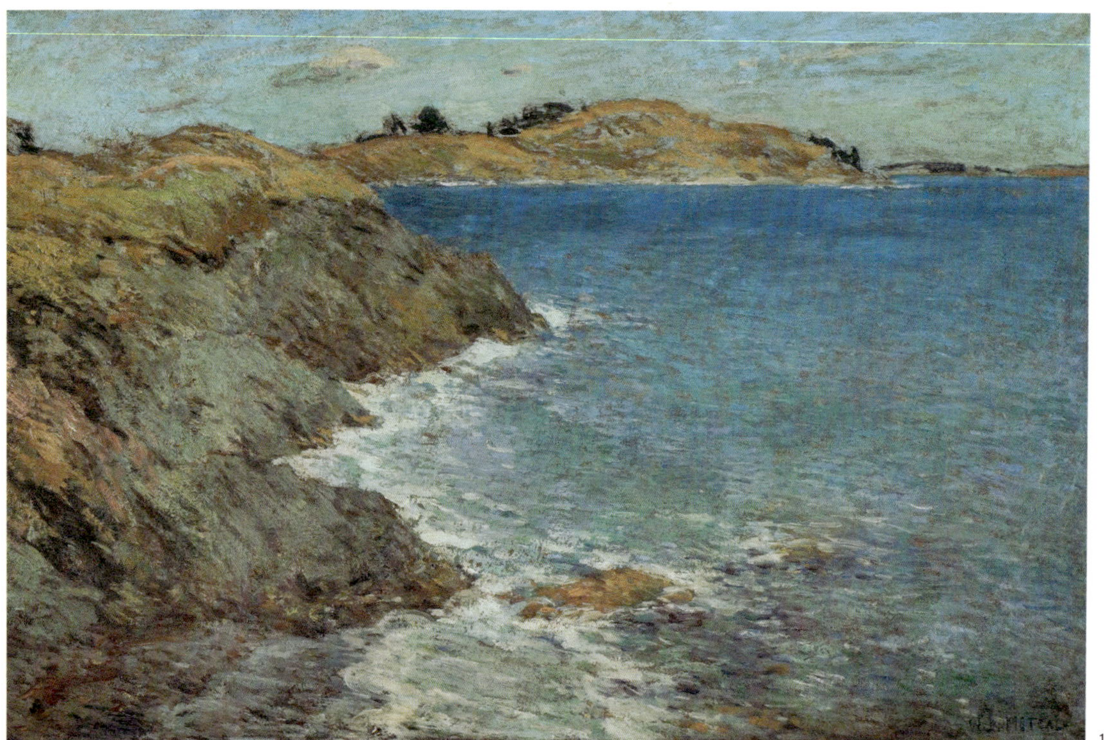

1

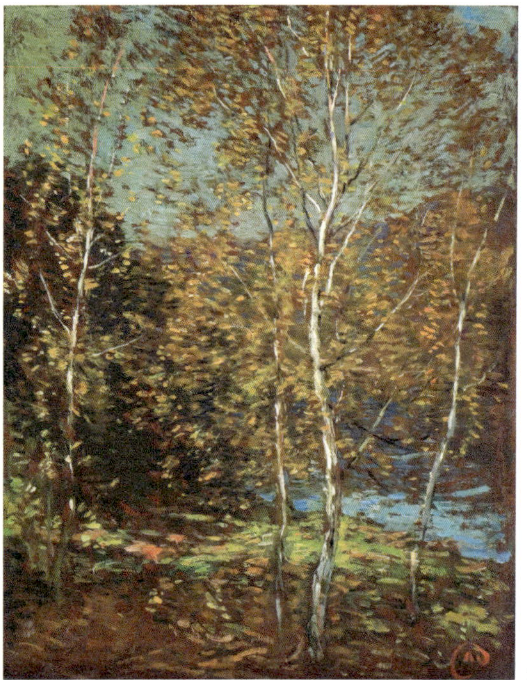

2

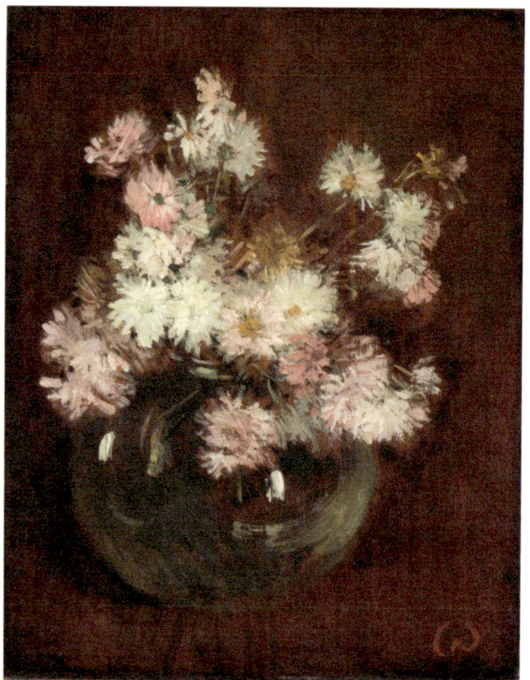

3

1 *Maine Coast*, 1907–08, Willard Metcalf
2 *Birches*, 1907–08, Willard Metcalf
3 *Chrysanthemums*, 1907, Willard Metcalf

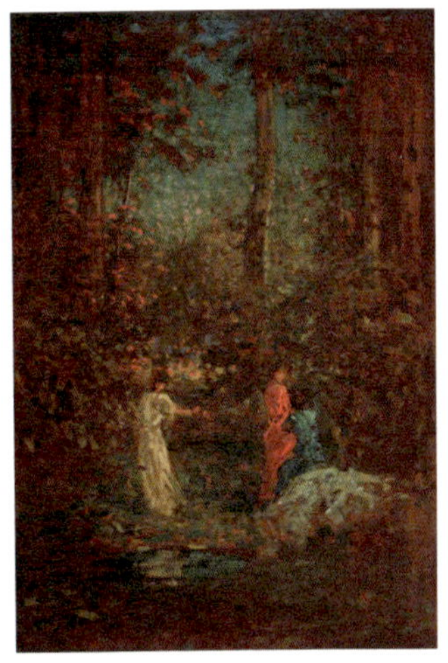
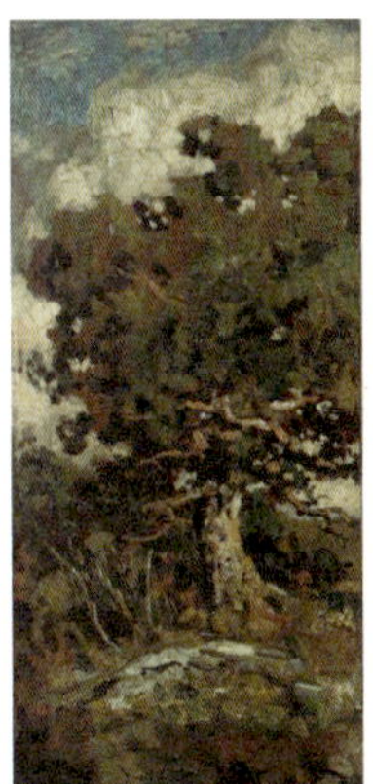
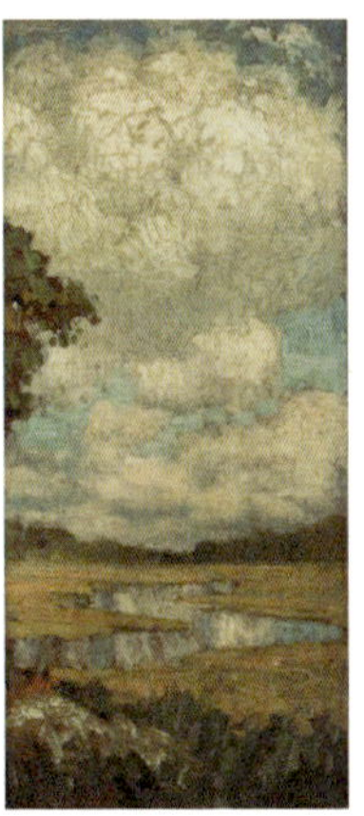
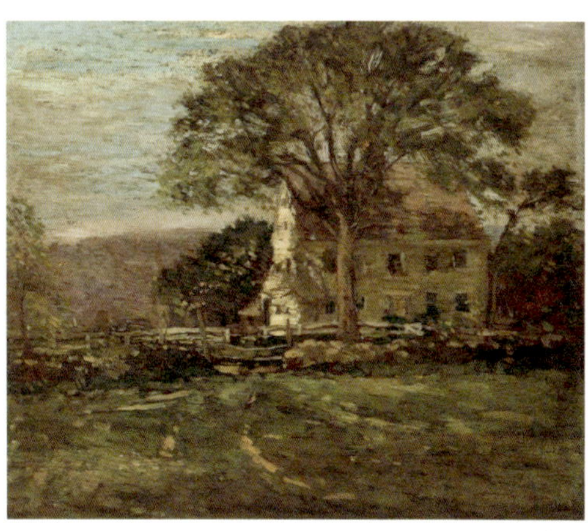
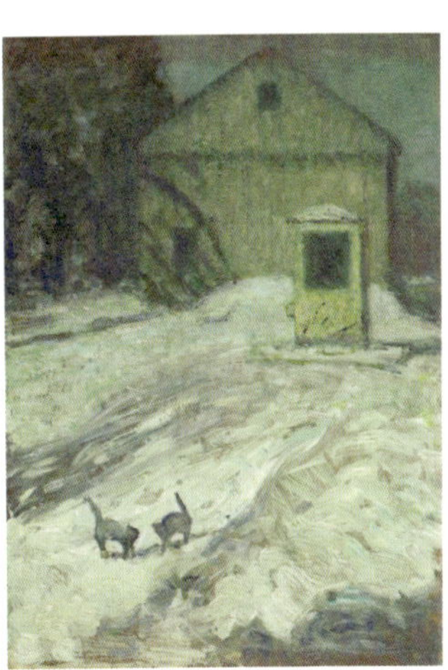
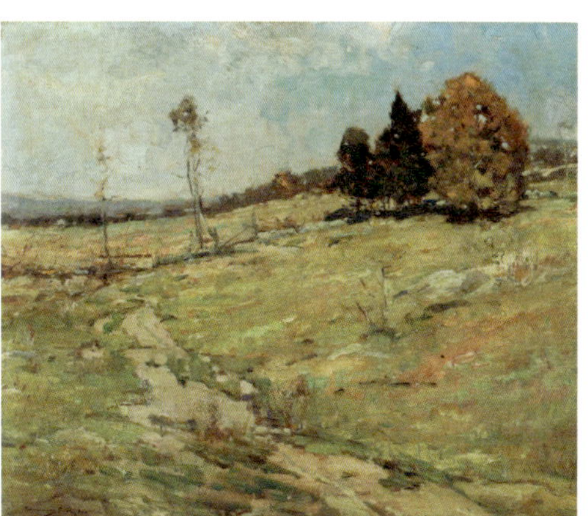

4 *Three Women in Woods*, Robert Nisbet

5 *The Lyme Marshes*, Allen Butler Talcott

6 *Spring—An Old House in Lyme*, 1905, William S. Robinson

7 *Kittens in the Snow*, Gregory Smith

8 *Autumn*, Chauncey Foster Ryder

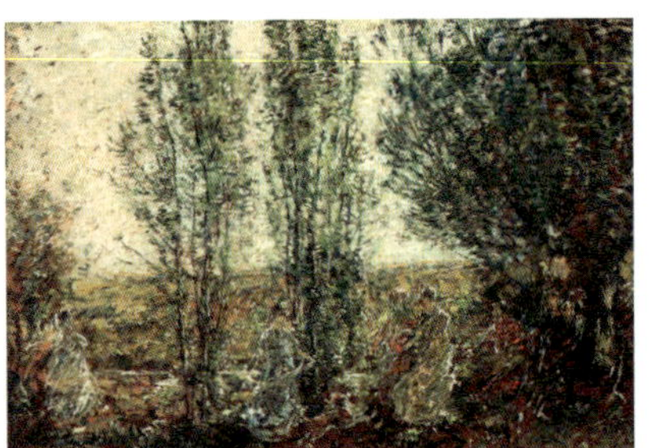 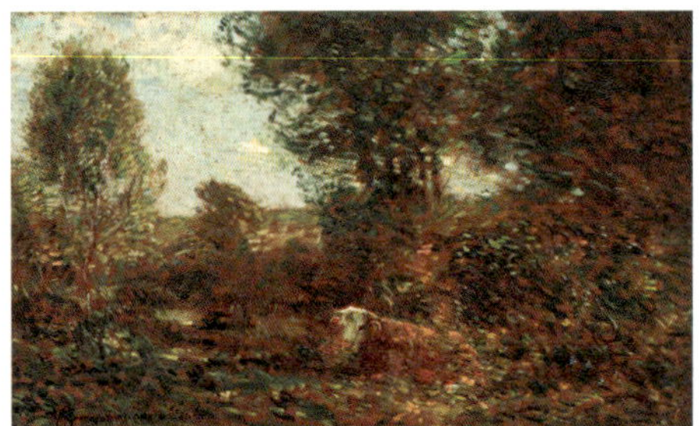 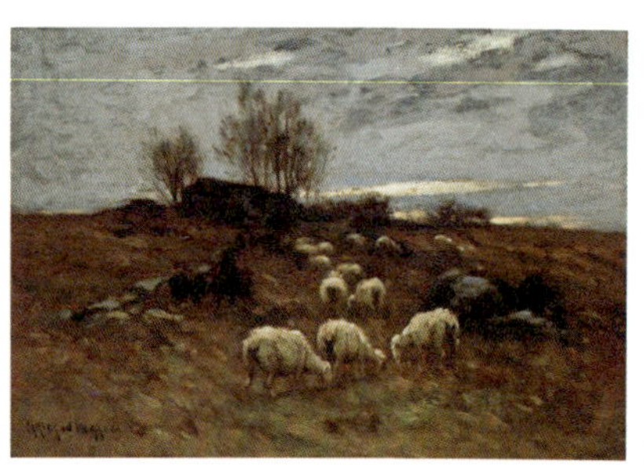

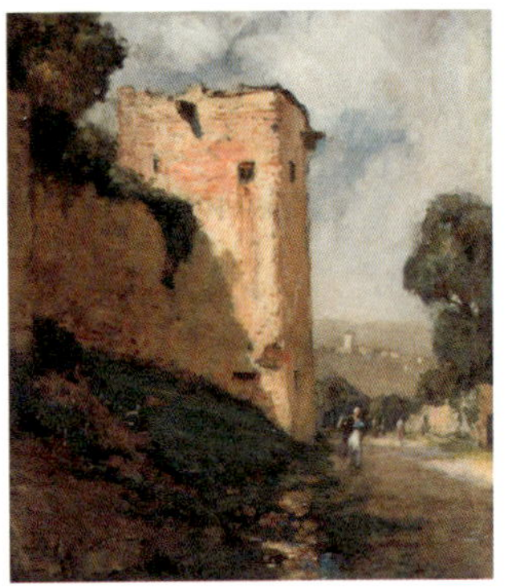 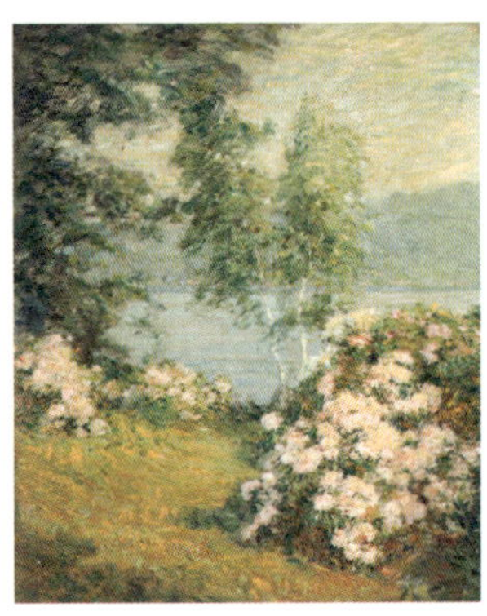 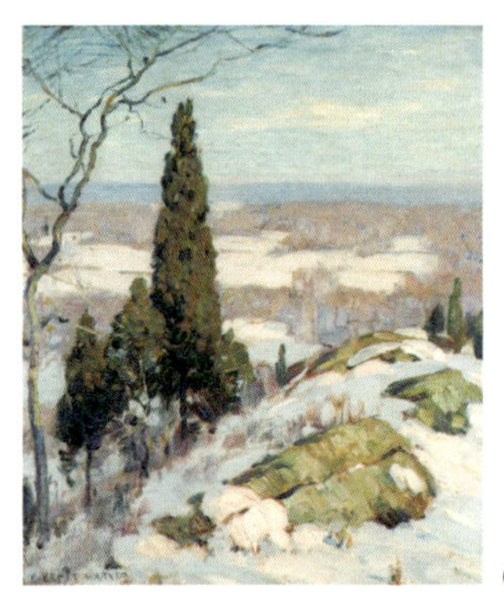 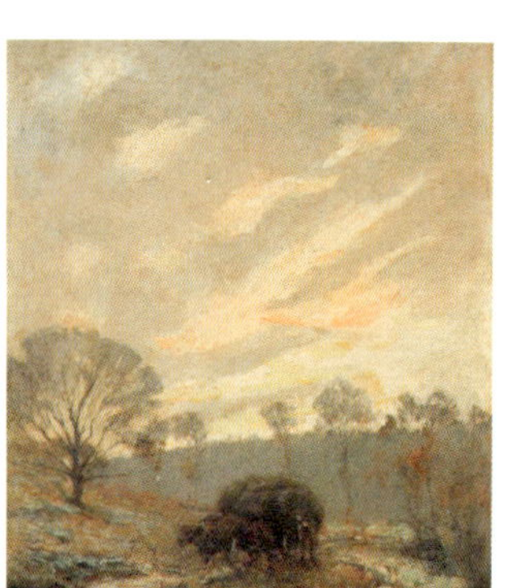

1 *Birches*, Walter Griffin

2 *Landscape with Cow*, 1907, Walter Griffin, Childe Hassam, Henry Rankin Poore

3 *Sheep*, Carleton Wiggins

4 *View of Granada*, 1910, Lewis Cohen

5 *Mountain Laurel*, 1910, Frank Bicknell

6 *Lyme in Winter*, Everett Warner

7 *Sunset Glow*, Jules Turcas

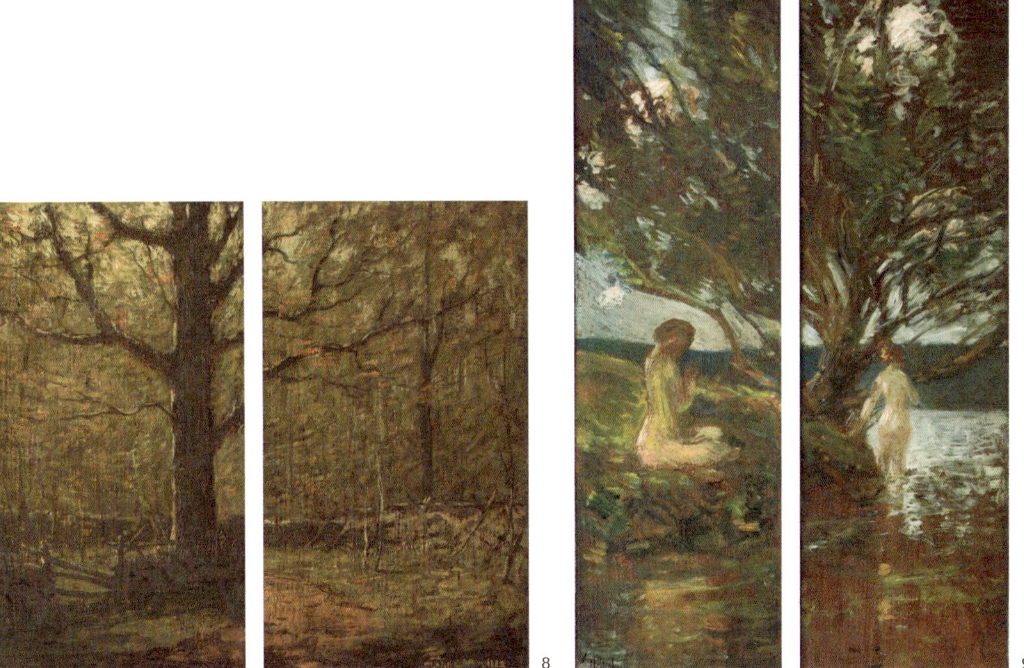

8 *Whippoorwill Road*, Clark Voorhees
9 *The Bathers*, 1903, Childe Hassam

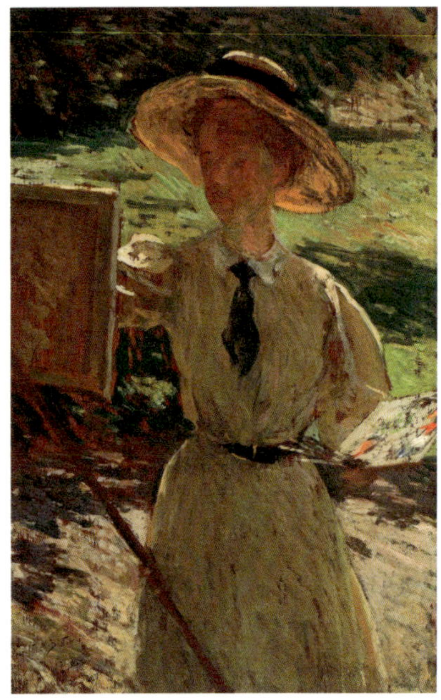

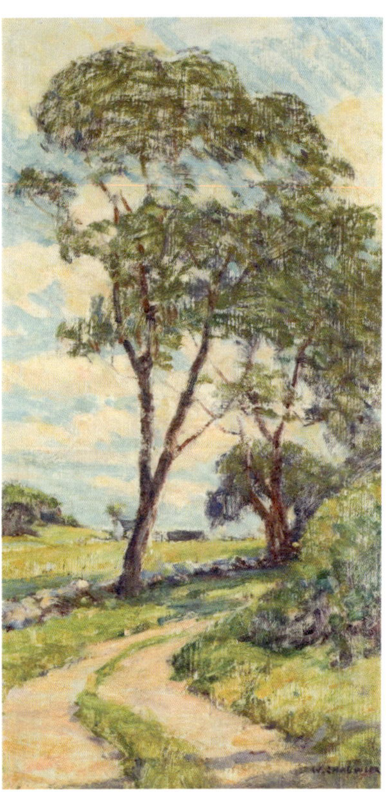

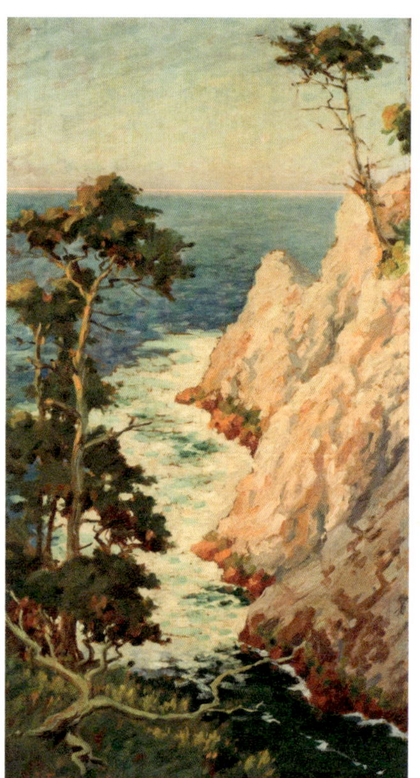

1 *Poor Little Bloticelli (Portrait of Lois Wilcox)*, 1907, Willard Metcalf

2 *Country Road in Summer*, William Chadwick

3 *Rocky Seacoast*, Robert Fullonton (hidden panel on reverse of Chadwick)

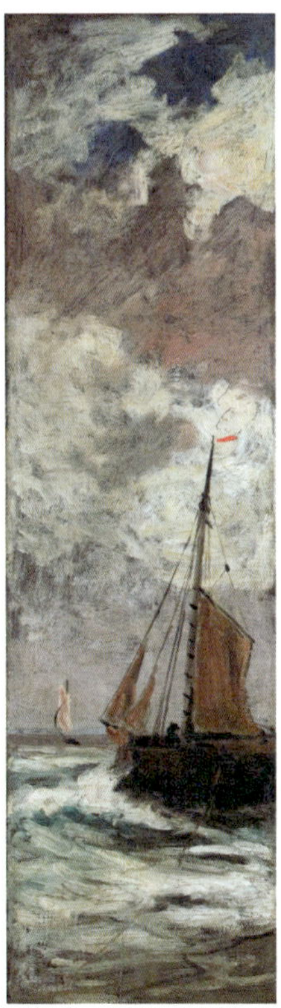
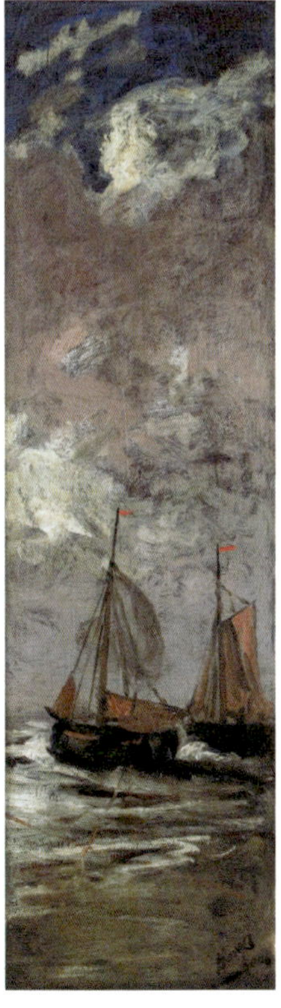
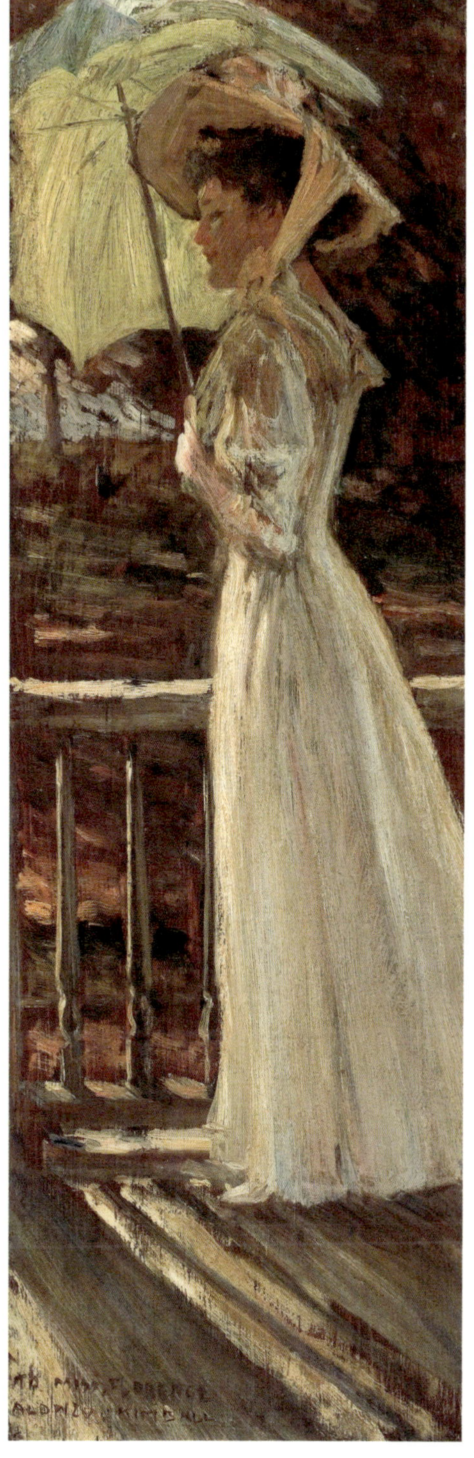

4 *Dutch Fishing Boats*, William Henry Howe
5 *Woman in White Dress and Pink Hat*, Alonzo Kimball

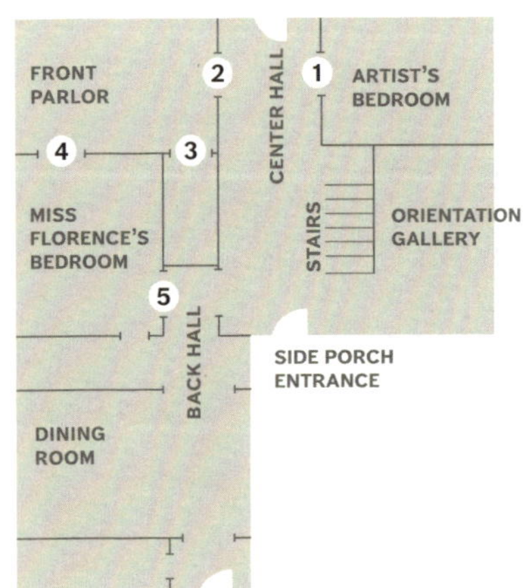

LOCATION OF PAINTED DOORS OUTSIDE OF THE DINING ROOM.

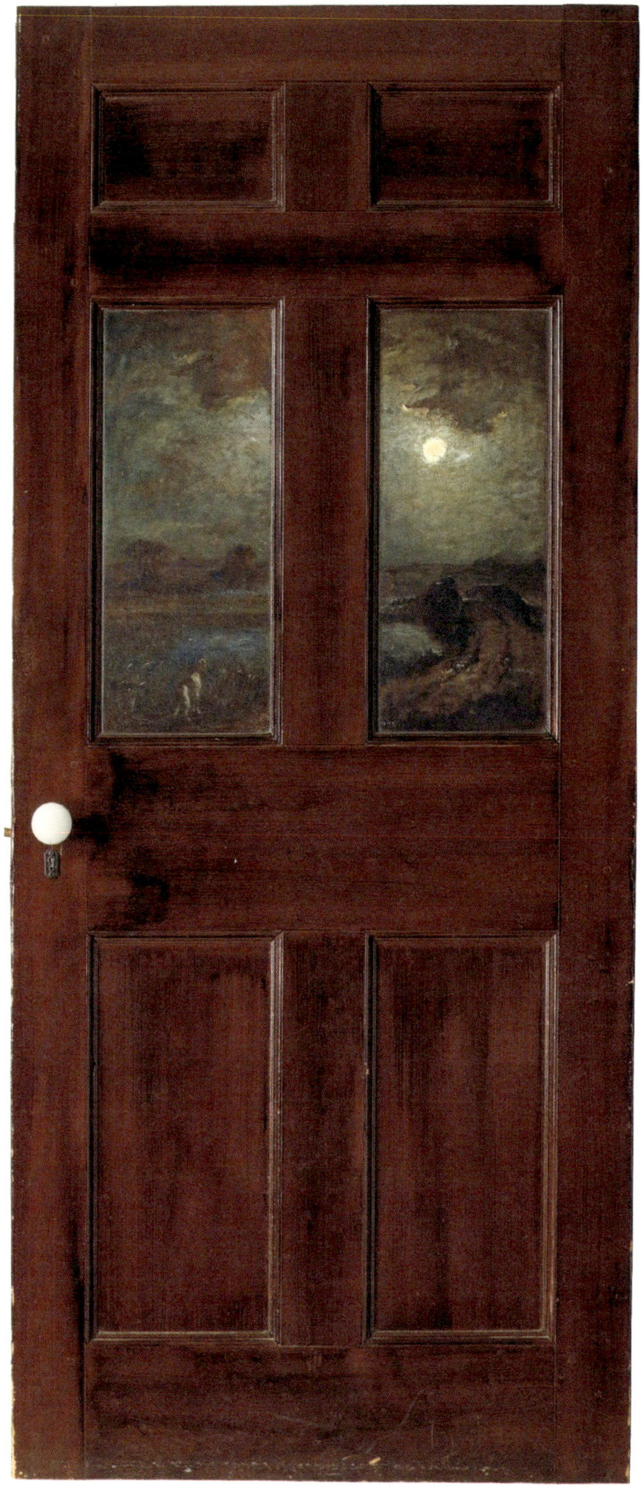

1   *Hound Dog Baying at Moon*, ca. 1901, Henry Rankin Poore
Bow Bridge by Moonlight, ca. 1901, Henry Ward Ranger

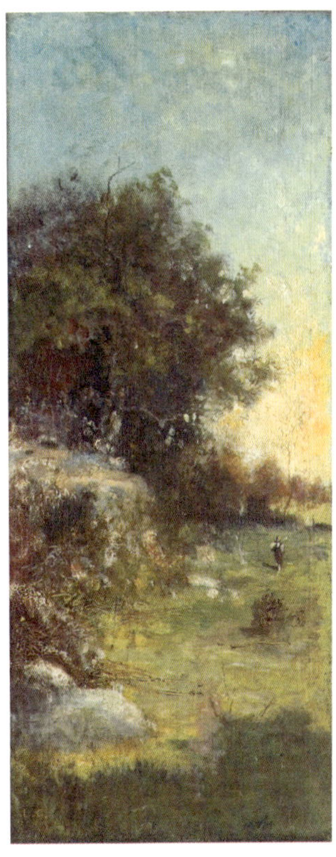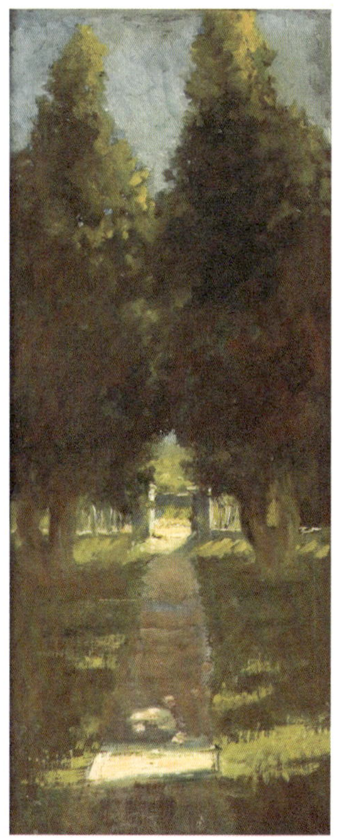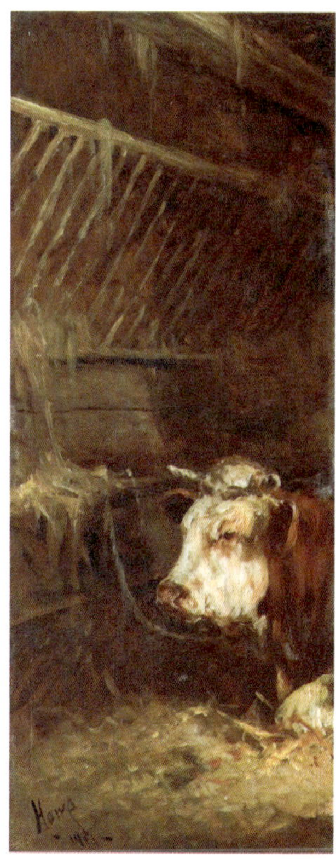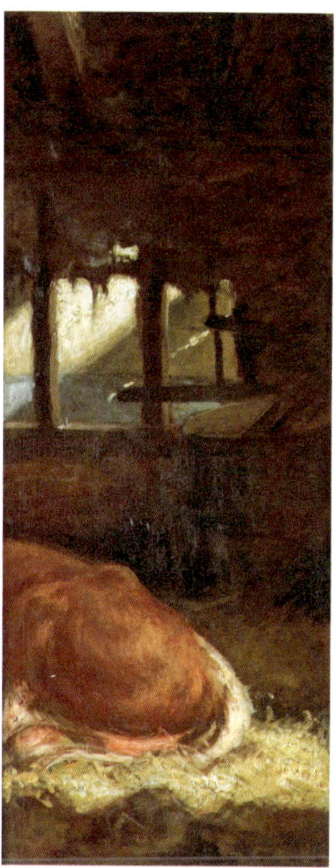

2 *Woods Near the House*, Lewis Cohen
Looking Down to the Front Gate, Lewis Cohen
3 *Normandy Stable*, 1901, William Henry Howe

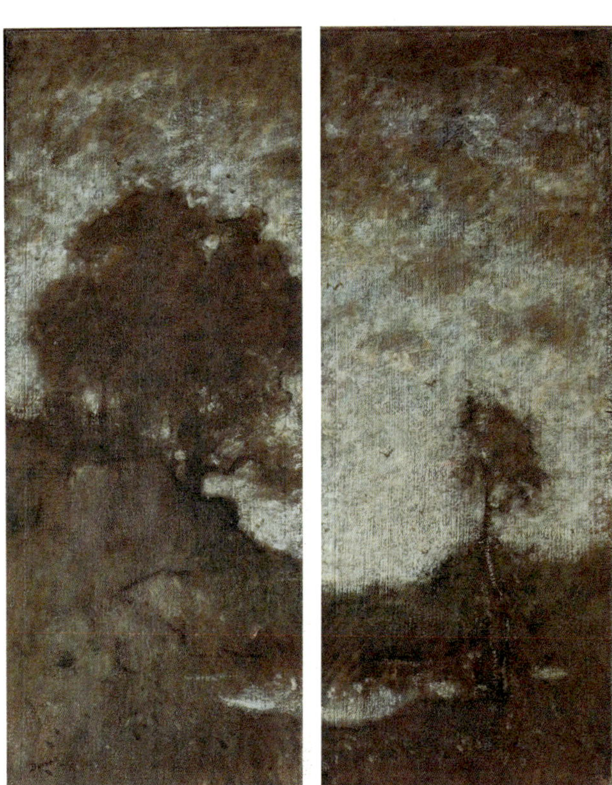

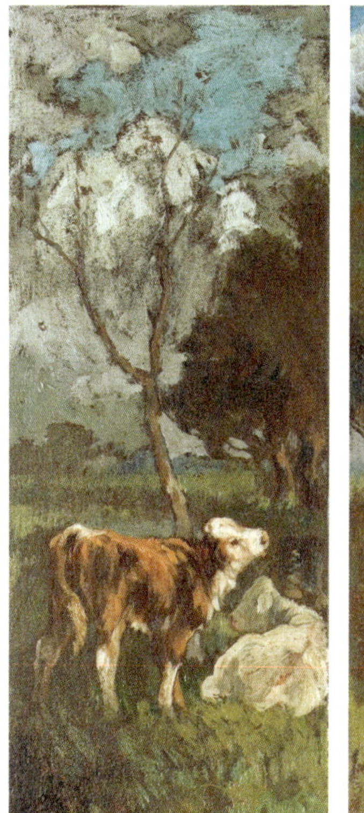

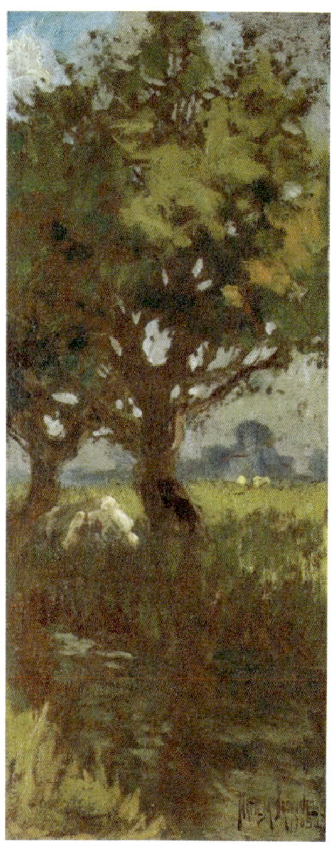

4   *Autumn Landscape*, Louis Paul Dessar
5   *Bucolic Landscape*, 1905, Matilda Browne

WITH THANKS

Over the years, the families of the artists of the Lyme Art Colony
featured in this story have been instrumental to the development of
the Florence Griswold Museum. Since the Museum's inception in 1936,
the Lyme artists and, more recently, their descendants have left an
indelible imprint on the Museum through their willingness to lend works
of art for exhibitions, make gifts to the collection, and become involved
as donors and trustees. Time and again, we have turned to the families of
these artists for advice and help in realizing our objectives. This second
edition of *Miss Florence and the Artists of Old Lyme* is a reminder of
how this legacy of participation extends from one generation to the next.

It gives us great pleasure to sincerely thank Nelson H. White for
his generous support of this book. Nelson is the third generation of
a distinguished family of artists that includes his father Nelson C. White,
whose original foreword appears in this book, and his grandfather
Henry C. White, who first brought his family to Old Lyme in 1903.
We also thank David J. Hoffman, the son of John L. and Margaret Hoffman
and the grandson of the Lyme artists Harry and Beatrice Hoffman, for
his support and for his family's role in preserving original records that
document the colony and highlight the close friendship that existed
between Harry Hoffman and Arthur Heming. This book is dedicated to
the lasting memory of all the artists of Old Lyme whose contributions
we honor at the Florence Griswold Museum.

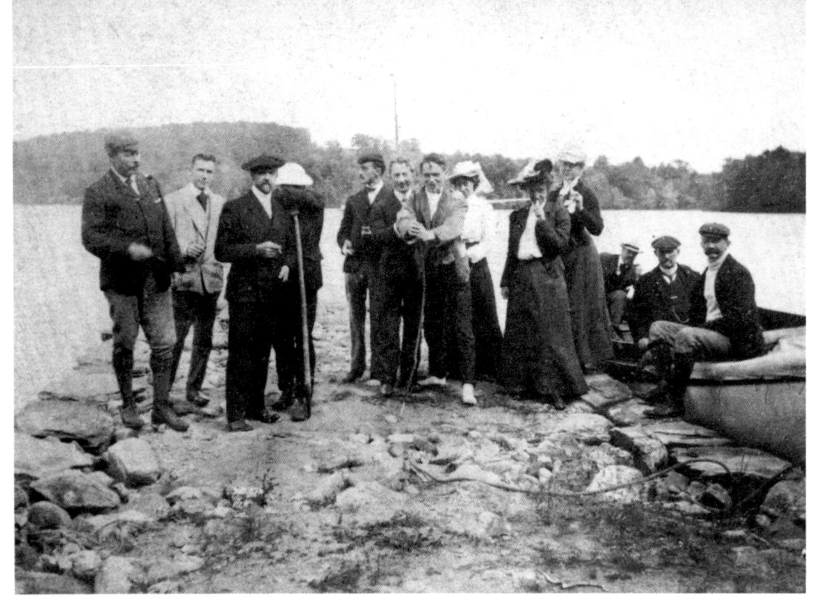

Lyme Art Colony picnic party, with Arthur Heming sixth from left and Florence Griswold in white blouse, ca. 1903. Lyme Historical Society Archives, Florence Griswold Museum.

About the Museum

The Florence Griswold Museum is a unique destination combining art, history, and nature on eleven acres along the Lieutenant River in the historic town of Old Lyme, Connecticut. Known as the Home of American Impressionism, the site is recognized for its role in American art history as the place where the members of the Lyme Art Colony lived and worked. Visitors to the site immediately appreciate its appeal to the artists who once stayed at Miss Florence's boardinghouse. In addition to the restored Florence Griswold House, the Museum features a gallery for changing art exhibitions, education and landscape centers, extensive gardens, and a restored artist's studio.

FlorenceGriswoldMuseum.org.